Activity Book 4

Jaap Tuinman

Maureen Neuman   Sharon Rich

CONSULTANTS

Sharon Anderson
Elaine Baker
John Drysdale
Julie Kniskern
Joanne McCabe
Claudia Mitchell
Kathleen Rosborough

PROGRAM EDITOR

Kathleen Doyle

Ginn and Company
Educational Publishers

Activity Book 4

EDITORS
Susan Green
Anne MacInnes
Janis Pellegrini
Sharon Stewart

EDITORIAL CONSULTANT
Nicki Scrimger

DESIGN
Helmut Weyerstrahs

Acknowledgments
Every reasonable precaution has been taken to trace
the owners of copyrighted material and to make due
acknowledgment. Any omission will be gladly rectified
in future editions.

C97486
ISBN 0-7702-1207-7

Printed and bound in Canada by
The Alger Press Limited
BCDEFG 93219089

Contents

Beasts, Birds, Bugs, and Us

Whoopers and Whoppers and Would You Believe It?

The Hoboken Chicken Emergency
Could Dracula Live in Woodford?

Weather or Not

Paint It! Weave It! Carve It!

O Canada!

Amos & Boris & Paddington Too

JOURNEYS

You and Me

Friends and Family

1. Sing this song with other children in your class.

    ♩♩ The more we get together, together, together,
    The more we get together, the happier we'll be... ♫

Then think of other songs about being friends.
Practise one of the songs and sing it for your class.

2. Imagine that you have moved to a new neighborhood
and a new school. With a partner, list all the things you could do
to meet people and make new friends.
Share your list with your class.

3. What is the most important rule for being a friend?
Ask at least ten people this question and tape-record what
they say.
Be sure to talk to people of all ages to get their ideas.
Play your tape for your classmates.

4. With some friends talk about some funny things that happen
when you and the other people in your family are rushing about
getting ready for work and school.
Choose some of the situations you discussed and act them out
for your class.

5. Write an acrostic poem about a friend.
Write a word beginning with each of the letters in *friend*.
Your poem could be serious or funny.
Here are two examples of
acrostic poems.

Faithful   **F**unny
Ready   **R**oly-poly
Interesting   **I**mpossible
Eager   **E**xhausting
Nice   **N**utty
Dependable   **D**opey

The children will: ☐ choose to complete unit activities

6. There are many poems about being part of a family.
Find some family poems and put your favorite ones into a book.
Read some of your favorite poems to your family.

 7. Work with a partner. Look through magazines and newspapers
to cut out pictures of families.
Arrange your pictures on a chart and make up a title for it.

 8. Make a family mobile. Draw a picture of each person in your
family. Then write words that tell about each person and attach
them with string to the picture.

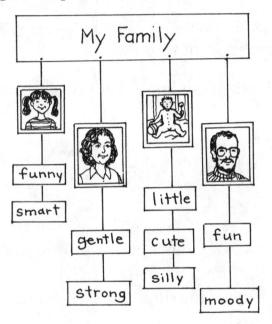

 9. Write all the words that come to your mind when you think of
family. Which ones can you group together?
Make a chart or web to show how you would group them.

 10. Find a book in the library about family or friends. Here are
some you might enjoy reading.

> *Aldo Ice Cream,* by Johanna Hurwitz.
> *Beezus and Ramona,* by Beverly Cleary.
> *Goodbye Sarah,* by Geoffrey Bilson.
> *It's a Good Thing,* by Joan Buchanan.
> *The Pinballs,* by Betsy Byars.
> *Superfudge,* by Judy Blume.

What Makes a Good Photograph?

What do you notice about the photographs?
Which photo in each row do you like better? Why?

The children will: ☐ observe to note details   ☐ compare to evaluate photos

Look at the cartoon story with a friend. Draw the missing part.
Tell each other the story.

Add another ending to the story. Draw pictures to show what happened.
Share your cartoon story with your friends.

The children will: ☐ interpret to note sequence

A Combination of Chris and Tina

Read the story.

Chris and I have always been best pals. We root for the same baseball team and we're both crazy about monster movies. We even like the same jokes. But when Mr. Teasdale asked for a volunteer to be editor of our class newspaper, I was really surprised when Chris shot his hand up. Mine was already up.

"Why are YOU volunteering?" I hissed. "I'm a lot better writer than you are."

"Yeah, but running a paper takes organization," Chris smirked. "And YOU couldn't organize your way out of a paper bag."

Mr. Teasdale said we'd have to campaign and let the class elect one of us.

At lunch, Chris munched his peanut butter sandwich and started making a list— Mr. Organization. I munched my peanut butter sandwich and searched for inspiration.

That night I got a bright idea. I made up some posters with snappy slogans about what a great editor I'd be.

Next morning, Chris beat me to school and put up a lot of posters, with funny pictures of himself. At recess, he went around talking to everyone. What a politician! Me, I couldn't do it. I'd feel phony and get tongue-tied.

After school I went to lie down in the hammock, hoping for more inspiration. I looked across to the backyard next door and saw Chris lying in a hammock too. Probably making another list, I thought.

The campaign went on all week. I wrote limericks. Chris drew cartoons. I taped a campaign jingle and played it for the class. Chris made about a million paper airplanes with his name on them and handed them out at recess. I wrote an article about the kinds of things I'd put in the newspaper. Chris did a layout of what the paper would look like.

Would you believe it—the election was a draw! So Mr. Teasdale suggested that we share the job. We call our paper "The ChrisTina Times."

TINA'S TOPS !!!!!

Tina knows what to do
To publish a paper for you
News, features, and sports
Tina reports.
Vote Tina and find out what's new.

To find out what's new
Give Tina a try.
She'll report on who
Did what where
when and why.

Make a web to show what each character is like.

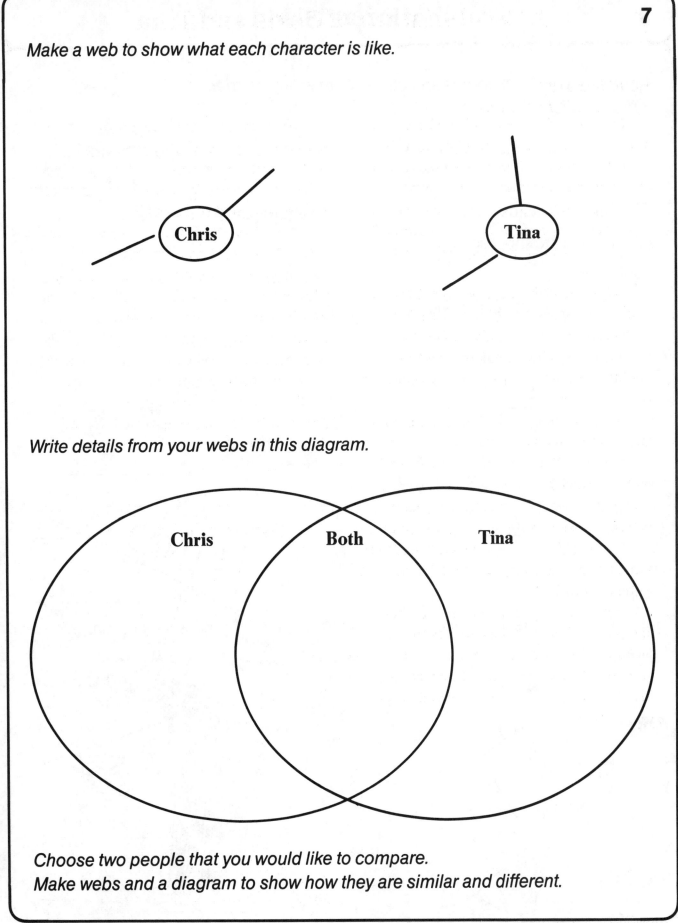

Write details from your webs in this diagram.

Chris   Both   Tina

Choose two people that you would like to compare.
Make webs and a diagram to show how they are similar and different.

The children will: ☐ web to compare characters   ☐ diagram to synthesize comparisons

My Friends and I

Complete your own poems and share them with your friends.
Write titles for your poems.

_____

_____

We could be friends
Like friends are supposed
   to be.
You, picking up the telephone
Calling me

_____

_____

_____

_____

_____

_____

Me, picking up the telephone
Calling you.

_____

_____

I went to play with _____ .

_____

_____

I _____

_____

_____

I _____

_____

_____

I _____

_____

A true good friend is a lot of fun.

The children will: ☐ imitate to create poems

Make a list of words that go with each of these words.

foggy	beach	water	gurgle	gull
_____	_____	_____	_____	_____
_____	_____	_____	_____	_____
_____	_____	_____	_____	_____
_____	_____	_____	_____	_____
_____	_____	_____	_____	_____
_____	_____	_____	_____	_____

Arrange the words in a web or a chart, or draw a shoreline and arrange groups of words where you think they belong.
Illustrate your web, chart, or diagram and show it to a friend.

The children will: ☐ list to associate related words ☐ web, draw, or chart to relate concepts

Jot down ideas in the left column. Write answers in the right column.

1. Why were DeDe and Aldo friends?

_____   _____
_____   _____
_____   _____
_____   _____
_____   _____

2. Why did the boys keep taking Aldo's egg?

_____   _____
_____   _____
_____   _____
_____   _____
_____   _____

3. What did you like about "A Fuss over Eggs"?

_____   _____
_____   _____
_____   _____
_____   _____

4. Who would you rather have for a friend, DeDe or Aldo? Why?

_____   _____
_____   _____
_____   _____
_____   _____

The children will: ☐ jot and arrange to organize answers

Read the paragraph and think of words that could go in the blanks.

"OK," he agreed. "I'll bring an egg tomorrow." Yet afterward, __1__ home toward Hillside Lane, Aldo felt he had __2__ too quickly. He should have said that he would bring an egg to school only on condition that she __3__ why she wore her __4__ moustache. Aldo was __5__ to get used to it like the other kids in the class. But still he was __6__ about why she wore it.

List possible words that would make sense for each blank.

1	2	3

4	5	6

Share your words with a partner. Then read the paragraph on page 13 of "A Fuss over Eggs" to find the exact words the author used. Write the exact words in the boxes.

The children will: ☐ hypothesize to predict and confirm word choice

Compare the Fare

Complete the chart to show how the stories are the same and different.

Questions	A Fuss over Eggs	The Sandwich
Who were the main characters?		
Who were the other characters?		
What was the problem?		
How was the problem solved?		
How did the main characters feel at the end?		
How do you think the other characters felt?		

Discuss your chart with your friends.

The children will: ☐ interpret to discriminate real and make-believe ☐ jot to justify opinions ☐ write to create news items

Complete the verses to make your own poem.   *Write a title for your poem.*

_____

"A person needs
A pal alot,

_____

_____

So thank you. Thank you."
There, it's said!

_____

_____

But even though
You're such a jerk,

_____

_____

I'm sort of glad
You're my old pard.

_____

_____

And I think those missing
Teeth are keen:

_____

_____

And every time
I see you grin,

_____

_____

You choke me up,
You make me sneeze,

_____

_____

Cause some things last and
Some things end—

_____

_____

Share your verses with your friends.

The children will: ☐ write to complete a poem

For Laura and Janey

Complete the chart to show how "Janey" and "For Laura" are the same and different. Share your answers with your classmates.

	For Laura	**Janey**
Form - story, poem, letter? - verses or paragraphs? - rhyme or no rhyme?		
Audience - Who is the author writing to?		
Purpose - Why is the author writing? - What part of the poem tells why?		
Feelings - What feelings does the poet express?		
Memories - How many?		
Pictures - What pictures does the poet make you see?		

The children will: ☐ chart to compare poems

Write and draw what might happen next.
Share your cartoon story with your friends.

The children will: ☐ illustrate to predict outcomes ☐ talk to share and compare ideas

Work with a partner to list situations when you might say the words in the boxes. Then say the words in tones of voice that would fit each situation.

You did it	Give it to me

What's going on in each picture? What might the children be saying?
Write the dialogue for each picture with a partner. Then act out the pictures, using your dialogues.

The children will: ☐ list to identify and share situations ☐ role-play to convey interpretation

Punctuate these quotes to show the meaning and feeling that you think each child is expressing.

What bugs me about families is visiting relatives ☐ We always end up going when there are really neat shows on TV ☐ My parents say it's selfish to ask for the shows I like ☐ So guess what happens ☐ I end up watching what they want to see ☐ Boring ☐

Yeah, I agree ☐ But you know what bugs me even more ☐ Relatives always ask the same dumb questions ☐ How do you like school ☐ What are you going to be when you grow up ☐ Yuck ☐

I don't agree one little bit ☐ My uncle lives with us and he doesn't do any of that stuff ☐ He plays around with me after supper and does sneaky things for me ☐ You know what he does when we're eating supper ☐ When no one's looking he scrapes my spinach onto his plate ☐ I hate spinach ☐

Compare your punctuation with a partner.

The children will: ☐ interpret to punctuate sentences ☐ compare to proofread for punctuation

Family Matters

Ask another child these questions. Check the boxes to show the answers. Work with your classmates to make a tally chart for the answers to each question.

1. Do you have problems with your brothers or sisters?
   ☐ Yes   ☐ No

2. Which of these people causes most of your problems?
   ☐ an older brother
   ☐ a younger brother
   ☐ an older sister
   ☐ a younger sister

3. Which of these situations causes most of the problems?
   ☐ watching TV programs
   ☐ borrowing things without permission
   ☐ winning or losing a game
   ☐ not paying back money
   ☐ breaking or losing things
   ☐ breaking a promise
   ☐ being late
   ☐ not sharing

4. When do most of your problems happen?
   ☐ after school
   ☐ after dinner
   ☐ on Saturday
   ☐ on Sunday

5. How do you usually solve your problems?
   ☐ fighting
   ☐ talking
   ☐ asking parents to help
   ☐ asking brother or sister to help

The children will: ☐ survey to research information ☐ graph to organize ideas

Reread the photo essay to write captions for the photographs.

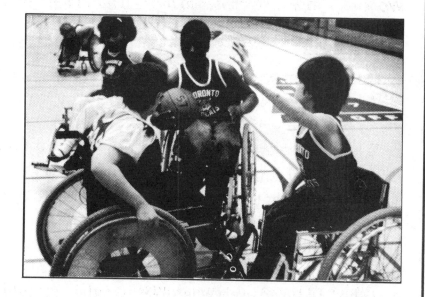

_____

_____

_____

_____

_____

_____

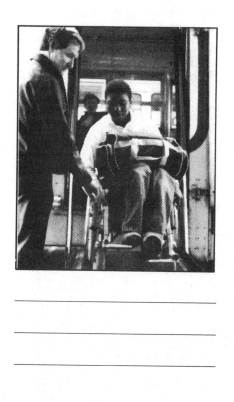

_____

_____

_____

_____

_____

_____

_____

_____

_____

The children will: ☐ interpret to link prose to pictures

Nibble Dribble?

Read the story.

Friday, May tenth, started out <u>ordinary</u>. I went to school and then came home and went <u>straight</u> to my room. The first thing I <u>noticed</u> was my bedroom door was open and there was a chair <u>smack</u> in the middle of the doorway. I nearly <u>tumbled</u> over it. I ran to <u>check</u> Dribble's bowl. He wasn't there! I <u>hollered</u> out to my mom, but she couldn't hear me because Fudge was <u>banging</u> pots and pans together. I looked everywhere, even in the bathroom <u>cabinet</u>. No Dribble. I <u>figured</u> Fudge had taken him. I figured right!

Write synonyms for the underlined words.

ordinary   _____

straight   _____

noticed   _____

smack   _____

tumbled   _____

check   _____

hollered   _____

banging   _____

cabinet   _____

figured   _____

Share your synonyms with a partner. Try the synonyms in the sentences.
Do they make sense? Which synonyms sound best?

The children will: ☐ list to identify synonyms ☐ talk to compare and choose synonyms

What place do you connect with a special someone in your family?
What are the main parts of the place?
Write the name of the place and four main parts of it. Then list things that are in each part.

_____

_____ _____ _____ _____

Draw a picture of the place, showing where the things go.

The children will: ☐ visualize to identify and list details ☐ illustrate to organize details

Which Words?

*Read the paragraphs and think of words
that could go in the blanks.*

But still, Grandmama was sad, taking old clothes
out of the closet and ___1___ them into a big box.
Rhondy knew just what to do to make her ___2___. She went to her room and
put on the ___3___ earrings Grandmama had given her to play with, and she tied
the ___4___ tablecloth with the ___5___ hole in it around her ___6___. Then she rolled
up a piece of ___7___ and took it with her to Grandmama's room. But she didn't go
in, she ___8___ around the door.

List possible words that would make sense for each blank.

1	2	3	4

5	6	7	8

*Share your words with a partner. Then read the paragraphs on page 51 of
"Grandmama's Joy" to find the exact words the author used.
Write the exact words in the boxes.*

The children will: ☐ hypothesize to predict and confirm word choice

On Friday evening there was a special on TV, and Aldo's parents let him stay up until almost midnight. The next morning it was gray and bitter cold outside. Aldo snuggled under the covers in his new bedroom and slept later than he had ever slept before.

It was 11:30 when he finally got out of bed, and it was noon before he was dressed and had brushed his teeth. He went into the kitchen to fix himself something to eat. He found an open box of cold cereal on the table and poured some into a bowl. He cut up a banana on top and added milk. Just as he was finishing the cereal Karen and his mother walked into the kitchen with brown grocery bags in their arms.

"If you're finished eating, ___1___ can help us unload ___2___ car," said Mrs. Sossi. "___3___ bought enough food to ___4___ an army, but in ___5___ house I'll be lucky ___6___ it lasts a week."

___7___ reached for some bread ___8___ put two slices in ___9___ toaster. "What are you ___10___?" asked his mother. "Didn't ___11___ just eat?"

"That was ___12___," Aldo explained. "Now I'm ___13___ some lunch."

Karen giggled ___14___ went outside to get ___15___ bag of groceries from ___16___ car. "On second thought," ___17___ Mrs. Sossi, "maybe this ___18___ will only last over ___19___ weekend."

Lunch for Aldo ___20___ of two slices of ___21___ and two slices of ___22___ and a glass of ___23___ juice.

"Why don't you ___24___ the crusts?" asked Mrs. ___25___. "Don't tell me you ___26___ hungry!"

"I didn't want ___27___," said Aldo, "and besides, ___28___ want to feed them ___29___ the birds." He took ___30___ crusts from his plate ___31___ also the end slices ___32___ bread, which always got ___33___ in the bag anyhow, ___34___ broke them into little ___35___. Then he opened the ___36___ door by the kitchen ___37___ threw the crumbs out ___38___ the yard. Peabody came ___39___ stood by the door ___40___ out, but he stayed in the warm house.

The children will: ☐ hypothesize to predict and confirm word choice

After he closed the door, Aldo stood by the kitchen window and began counting. He had discovered that somewhere between the count of seventy and one hundred the birds would arrive when he put food out. First one came timidly hopping close to the offering, and then suddenly a dozen others appeared, all pushing and grabbing like his classmates on the lunch line. Aldo was fascinated by the birds and thought he could watch them all day long.

"Is there anything else we could give the birds?" Aldo asked. Then he remembered. "Did you buy some birdseed for the feeder?"

"They only had four-kilogram bags," said Mrs. Sossi, "and I had enough things to buy as it was. Maybe next week," she said, seeing her son's disappointed face.

"Well, can I throw out more bread?" begged Aldo.

"Enough is enough," argued Mrs. Sossi. "I have to worry about feeding our family and the cats. I can't assume responsibility for all the birds in the neighborhood too."

Aldo looked in the refrigerator and found a dish containing some leftover spaghetti from three nights before. "Is anyone going to eat this?" he asked.

"I doubt it," said his mother.

"Then I'll give it to the birds," said Aldo triumphantly. "They'll think it's a new kind of worm."

Adapted excerpt from pp. 55–58 "Fussing over the Birds" in *Aldo Applesauce* by Johanna Hurwitz, copyright © 1979 by Johanna Hurwitz. By permission of William Morrow & Company.

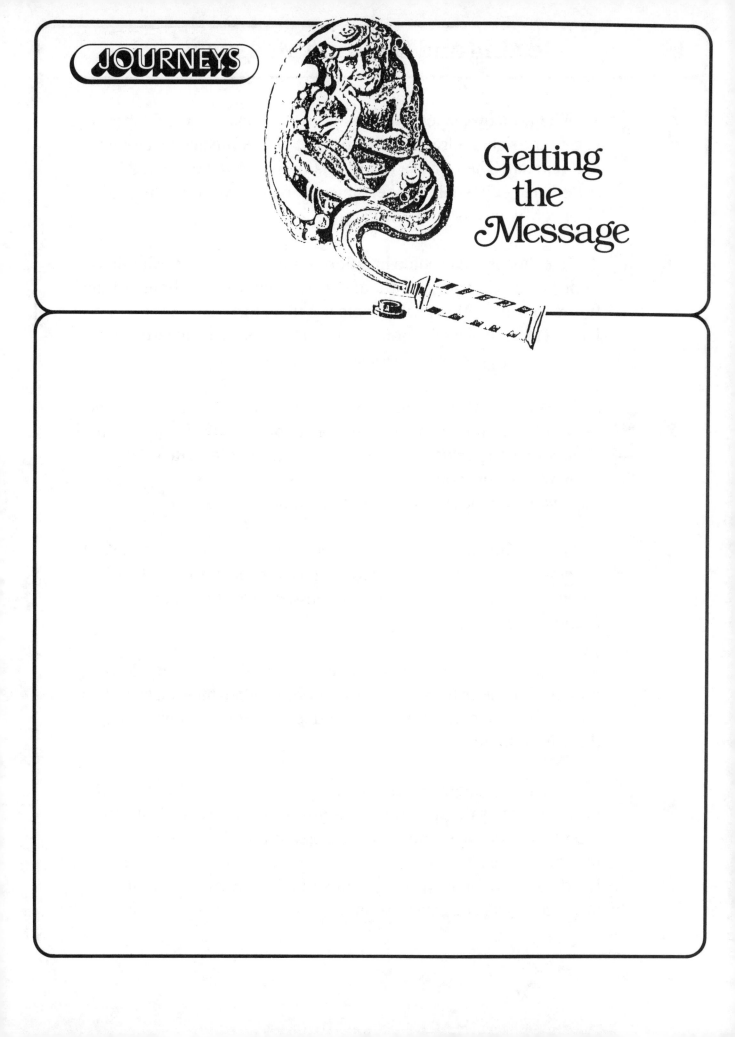

Getting the Message

1. When you drop a letter in a mailbox, do you ever wonder how it gets to the right address? Look up "Post Office" in an encyclopedia and find out. Then write a report on how letters get collected, sorted, and delivered. Use headings to organize your information. "Deliver" your report to the class.

 2. Telephones today come in different shapes and sizes, with dials or push buttons, with or without cords. What will telephones of the future look like? What will people use them for?
Draw a picture of a telephone of the future and write a description of how it works and what people can use it for.

 3. Look at some TV commercials or magazine advertisements and list words they use to persuade people to buy things. Then write a commercial to persuade people to eat your *least* favorite food, using words from your list. You could include a rhyme or a jingle. Tape your commercial and play it for some classmates.

 4. People often say "a picture is worth a thousand words." Think of a message you'd like to get across, such as "Don't be a litterbug." Draw a picture that expresses your message and show it to some friends. Do they get the message?

 5. Work with some friends to make a model of a city street. Make up some messages to put on store windows, office buildings, movie theatres, traffic poles, newspaper and mail boxes, and anything else that's in your model.

 6. Sounds without words can send very clear messages. What is the message sent by the siren on an ambulance or firetruck? Listen to sounds at home, at school, and in the street. Jot down or tape-record the sounds.
Read your list or play your tape for some friends and see what messages they get from the sounds.

The children will: ☐ choose to complete unit activities

7. People use gestures and body movements to send messages. How would you "say" these messages without using words: "Come here." "Go away." "This tastes delicious!"

Work with a partner or some friends to think up messages that you can send just with movements and gestures. Then act them out in front of the class.

8. What guesses would you make about the owner of these things?

- a library card
- a Scrabble game
- a bag with yogurt and an apple
- a terry cloth sweatband

Make a list or drawings of things that tell about you. Put them in an envelope marked "Return to Sender" and leave it on a friend's desk. Did your friend return the envelope to the right sender?

9. What will be news in the year 2000? With some friends, prepare a newspaper of the future. Each of you could supply different kinds of news—national news, world news, galaxy news, sports, science, entertainment.

You could print your news or "broadcast" it as a radio or TV program for the rest of your class.

10. Find a book in the library about sending or receiving messages. Here are some you might enjoy reading.

Basil and the Pygmy Cats, by Eve Titus.
A Button in Her Ear, by Ada Litchfield.
The Case of the Secret Scribbler, by E.W. Hildick.
A Clue in Code, by Marilyn Singer.
Communications from the Beginning, by Alma Gilleo.
Newspapers, by David Petersen.

Read the advertisement.

> **BICYCLE BARGAIN!**
>
> Girl's 5-speed bicycle with hand brakes for sale. Rapido. Just $57. In very good condition—nearly new. Call 672-1341.

Think of an article you would like to sell. Web the information you would include in an advertisement and then circle the most important details.

Write an advertisement for the article. Include the most important details and any information that you think would make someone want to buy the article.

_____

_____

_____

_____

_____

The children will:　□ web to record details　□ write to create an advertisement

Read the article and answer the questions.

Imagine a world without printed books. Imagine writing a novel or an encyclopedia or any book by hand. And then imagine having to write copies of any of these books by hand too. That's the way books were made up until five hundred years ago. No wonder there were so few books long ago!

And then all that changed because of an invention by a man named Johannes Gutenberg, who lived in Germany. Gutenberg's great idea was to make small blocks of metal with raised letters of the alphabet on them, one letter to each little block. These metal letters are called *type.* Gutenberg placed his metal blocks of letters side by side to make words and sentences, and then entire pages of type. Of course, he needed many sets of type to make up a book!

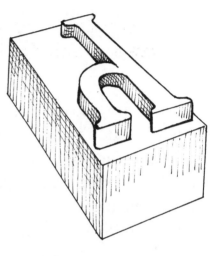

Gutenberg also invented a machine to hold his type. After he placed the type in the machine, he brushed it with ink. Then the machine pressed paper against the inky type, creating printed pages. As you may have guessed, Gutenberg's invention was the *printing press.*

You can see why the printing press was such an important invention. It could print many copies of the same book, and the metal type could be rearranged over and over to print many different books. So printers could produce many books quickly and easily. And as more and more books were printed, more and more people learned to read and write, and ideas spread faster and farther than ever before.

Think of all the libraries and book stores in Canada and around the world. Think of all the ideas in all the books, magazines, and newspapers in the world. And it all began with Gutenberg's invention of the printing press.

How did Gutenberg's invention change the way books were made?

Why was the invention of the printing press so important? Why is it important for you?

In what ways is the invention of radio and television like the invention of the printing press?

The children will: ☐ interpret to note, infer, and project information

There are codes, like Pig Latin and Iggity, that people use to exchange secret messages when they're talking. Here are some codes that people use to exchange secret written messages.

Some secret codes use letters of the alphabet. One kind of code scrambles the letters in words. Another kind substitutes different letters. In this message, each letter is replaced by the following letter in the alphabet: NFFU   NF   BU   UIF   QBSL. In this message, each letter is replaced by the preceding letter in the alphabet: RDD   XNT   SNMHFGS.

There are also codes that hide letters and words of secret messages. In one kind of hidden message code, the first letter of each word makes up the secret message. Can you read this one? *Sam expects either Yvonne or Uri to officially name Ira's giant hamster today.* In another kind, the words of the secret message are mixed in with other words. If you circle every fifth word in this message, you'll find the secret message: *Mary said the track meet is tomorrow. She told me we have to leave at eleven sharp to catch the express bus for the park.*

Other secret codes use numbers to replace letters. If you number the letters forward, then *A* is 1, *B* is 2, and so on. Using this number code, you would write the message MEET ME AT THE PARK this way: 13-5-5-20   13-5   1-20   20-8-5   16-1-18-11. You can also number the letters backward, so that *Z* is 1, *Y* is 2, and so on. Or you can give each letter any number you want to.

People also use books to pass secret messages. One way to code a message is to place a tiny dot under words or letters scattered through the book. Then you pass the book to the person who is supposed to read the message. Another way is to write numbers under the words or letters in two copies of the same book. Then you and a partner can each use your copy of the "code book" to exchange secret messages in numbers.

The children will: ☐ interpret and web to identify main ideas

Read what the first phone caller said.

1. Hi, is Paula there? Well, could I leave a message? Tell her I want to get together to work on our science project. Could she call me after 5:00? My number is 926-4913. Pardon? Oh—this is Sylvie. Bye!

   _____
   _____
   _____
   _____
   _____
   _____
   _____

2. Hi, this is Dave. May I please speak to Jerry? Oh. I need to know if he'll look after my pet turtle this weekend. Do you know when he'll be back? OK. Would you ask him to call me as soon as he gets in? What? Oh, it's 410-7100. Thanks.

   _____
   _____
   _____
   _____
   _____
   _____
   _____

Jot down the main points of the first phone call in the space beside it. Work with your group to make up a message form for recording the main points of a phone call.

Write the headings for your form in the space beside the second phone call. Test your form by reading the second phone call and writing the message on your form.

The children will: ☐ jot to note main points ☐ talk to create a message form ☐ write to organize a message

Which Words?

Read this part of the story and think of words that would fit in the blanks.

"What do you do when you ___1___ out?"

The tip of Shah's tail ___2___ back and forth. "I go for ___3___ stroll, check out the neighborhood, see ___4___ the other cats are up to, ___5___ catch a mouse—the usual sorts ___6___ things."

Shah was not a very ___7___ conversationalist, Amanda thought, but she persisted. "___8___ do you think about?"

"When?"

"Any ___9___. When you're chasing a mouse. Now."

"___10___ I'm chasing a mouse I'm thinking ___11___ chasing the mouse, or perhaps catching ___12___ mouse. Now I'm thinking I wish ___13___ stop asking questions." Shah noticed Amanda's ___14___ of disappointment and added in a ___15___ tone, "Look, I like living here. ___16___ a quiet family and feed me ___17___ and don't disturb me—much. And ___18___ mind my own business as I ___19___ everyone—cat or human—ought to ___20___."

Write a word that would fit and make sense for each blank.

1. _____	11. _____
2. _____	12. _____
3. _____	13. _____
4. _____	14. _____
5. _____	15. _____
6. _____	16. _____
7. _____	17. _____
8. _____	18. _____
9. _____	19. _____
10. _____	20. _____

Share your words with a partner. Then read the passage on pages 69–70 of "Parlez-vous français?" to compare the author's words with yours.

The children will: ☐ hypothesize to predict and confirm word choice

Write what you think each hand signal means.

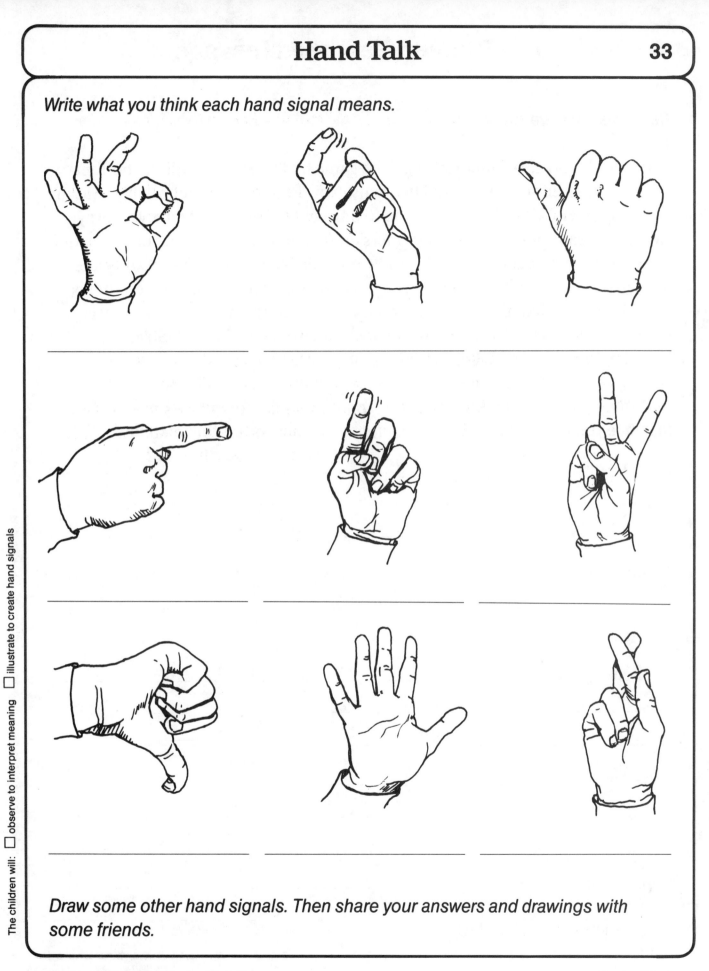

Draw some other hand signals. Then share your answers and drawings with some friends.

The children will: ☐ observe to interpret meaning ☐ illustrate to create hand signals

The Pitcher Gets the Message

Read the passage.

It was the top of the ninth inning. The game had been tied until the bottom of the eighth, when the Jays scored two runs. Now Renko, the relief pitcher, was in a tight spot. He'd come into the game to protect the lead, but he'd given away two hits already, and there were runners on first and third. The call on the batter stood at three balls and two strikes. The catcher crouched behind home plate and gave the signal. Renko nodded slightly and slowly brushed the front of his cap with his left hand. Then he wound up and threw the ball. The batter was ready, but just as he swung at the ball, it curved wickedly inward. Strikeout! The crowd went wild. Renko grinned. Good old curve ball!

Write the meaning each word has in the paragraph. Underline the context clues that give you the meaning. Write a sentence that shows another meaning.

1. tied—meaning: _____
   _____
   _____

2. relief—meaning: _____
   _____
   _____

3. pitcher—meaning: _____
   _____
   _____

4. batter—meaning: _____
   _____
   _____

5. plate—meaning: _____
   _____
   _____

The children will: ☐ interpret to identify meaning from context　☐ write to show meaning in a different context

Look at the pictures and number them in the right order. Then follow the hand movements in each step and make a plane.

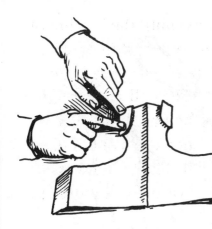

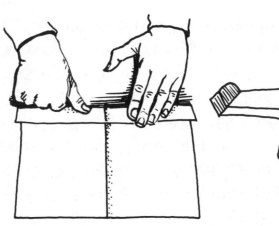

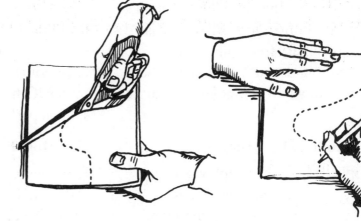

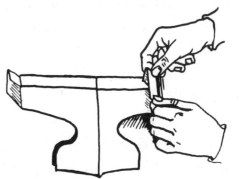

Read the article and work with a partner or your group to organize the information in a diagram.

There are many inventions and services to help blind people and deaf people to communicate.

Inventions to Help Blind People

One useful invention for the blind is the Kurzweil Reading Machine. This is a computer that is programmed to pronounce words. All a blind person has to do is place a book face down on the computer's glass screen and a robotlike voice reads the pages aloud. Many public libraries have Kurzweil machines. Another invention for the blind is the seeing-eye traffic signal. The signal is attached to ordinary traffic lights. It makes high-pitched sounds that tell a blind person when to walk or when to wait for the light to change.

Inventions to Help Deaf People

Deaf people can use the telephone now, thanks to two new inventions. One is a special receiver that makes spoken sounds louder. Another is the Visual Ear, which allows even totally deaf people to use the telephone. The Visual Ear is a keyboard and screen that can be attached to any telephone. The deaf person types a message on the keyboard, and the answer from the person at the other end appears in writing on the display screen.

Radio and Television Services

Radio and television help the blind and the deaf with special services. Radio for the Blind is a radio reading service. Volunteers come to the radio station and read newspaper articles and stories. Listeners can even hear

the comics! Television provides two kinds of services for deaf people. Some programs have printed captions at the bottom of the screen. Others show a person signing the spoken part of the program for deaf viewers.

How Dogs Help

Everyone knows that seeing-eye dogs are trained to lead their blind owners safely across busy streets and guide them away from other dangers. Now there are hearing-ear dogs to help deaf people. These dogs warn their owners of important sounds, such as ringing telephones and crying babies.

Organizations that Help

The Canadian National Institute for the Blind provides courses in Braille and helps blind people with education and job training. The Canadian Hearing Society organizes many services for the deaf, including lessons in signing. Because of these organizations, many blind or deaf people are able to live normal, useful lives.

The children will: ☐ diagram to organize information

Words that Make Pictures

Read the paragraph.

He kicked a rock across the street, hard. It skipped right past the beautiful mailbox with the door and the signal flag he and Perry always raised when they left messages for each other. But it was Mr. James's mailbox now, for his letters and mail. They'd have to find a new place to exchange notes and reports.

With your friends, talk about how the information in this paragraph is different from the information in the same paragraph on page 75 of "The Code in the Mailbox."

Read this paragraph and write possible describing words for each blank.

The Photo in the Attic

Jackie bent over the __1__ photograph she had found in the __2__ attic. It had a route marked on it! A dotted line passed between two __3__ hills and continued across a __4__ river with stepping-stones. Beyond the river, the photo showed a __5__ cliff, and at the bottom of the cliff was marked an X. Jackie shivered with excitement. Did the X mark a cave? A cave filled with __6__ treasure?

1. _____
   _____
   _____

2. _____
   _____
   _____

3. _____
   _____
   _____

4. _____
   _____
   _____

5. _____
   _____
   _____

6. _____
   _____
   _____

The children will: ☐ hypothesize to list descriptive words   ☐ compare to note descriptive words

Write a word that describes Louis Braille's character in each of the boxes. Under each characteristic write proofs from the article.

Louis
Braille

Which characteristic helped him most in inventing a system for blind people to read and write? Why do you think so?

The children will: ☐ chart to summarize characteristics and proofs

Write words that would fit in the poem you listened to.

1. _____ 4. _____

2. _____ 5. _____

3. _____ 6. _____

Read the verse and write words that would fit.

Word Parade

One-letter words march quickly by:

A walks alone, and so does _____.

Two-letter words prance merrily:

In and *at* and *it* and _____.

Three-letter words troop two by two:

Get with *old* and *yes* with _____.

Four-letter words strut in alone:

Star and *tale* and *flow* and _____.

Five-letter words skip all around:

Crisp and *knock* and *tight* and _____.

Six-letter words all trip and stumble:

Ramble, jagged, gobble, _____.

—SHARON STEWART

Share your words with some friends.

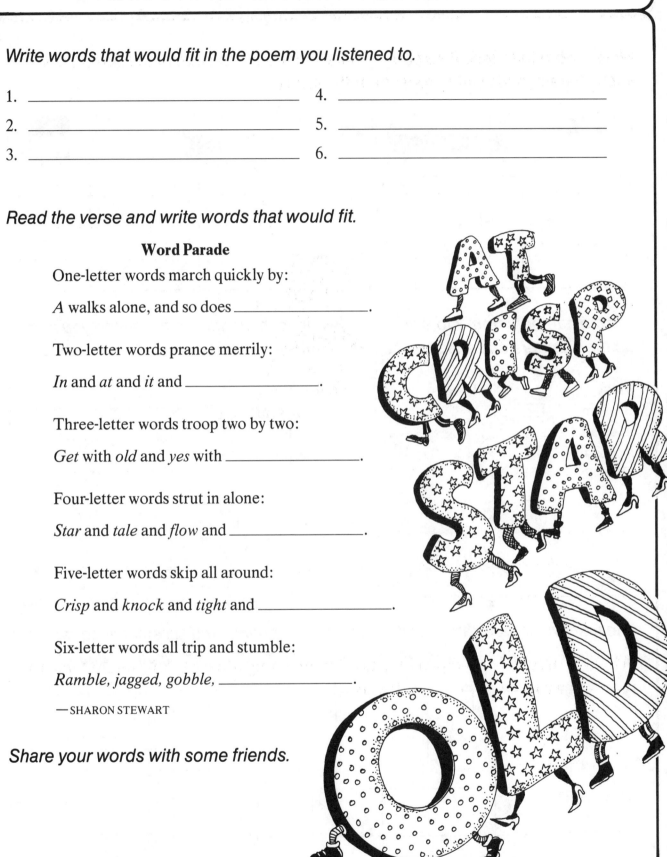

Continue the pattern.

102, 203, 304, _____ , _____ , _____ .

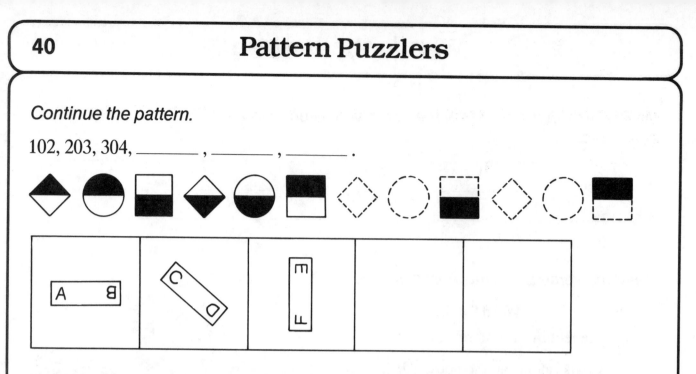

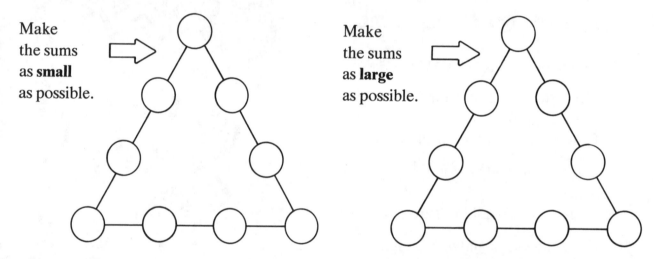

Put the numbers from 1 to 9 in the circles of each triangle so that when you add up the numbers on each side the three sums are all the same.

Make
the sums
as **small**
as possible.

Make
the sums
as **large**
as possible.

The first two squares are cut into four smaller squares and six smaller squares. Cut the other squares into seven smaller squares and eight smaller squares.

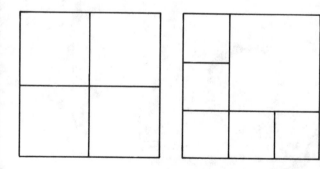

Draw more squares and keep on going.

The children will: ☐ interpret to note and extend patterns

Here are two more concrete poems you might enjoy. Read them and answer the questions.

Greedy

The Snail

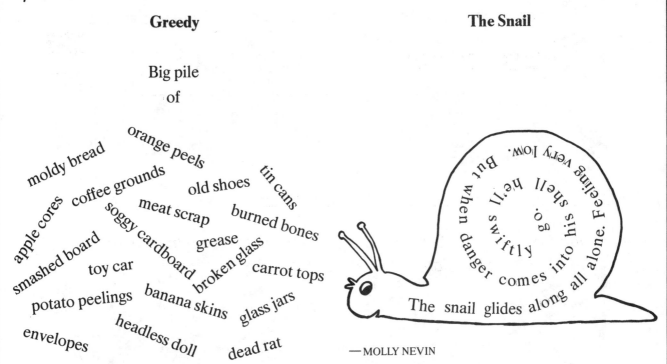

Big pile

of

moldy bread

orange peels

apple cores coffee grounds old shoes tin cans

meat scrap burned bones

soggy cardboard grease

smashed board

toy car broken glass carrot tops

potato peelings banana skins glass jars

envelopes headless doll dead rat

The snail glides along all alone. Feeling very low. But when danger comes into his shell he'll go swiftly

—MOLLY NEVIN

Here comes the garbage truck.

GOBBBBLLLLLE.

—ROBERT FROMAN

Which poem do you like better? Why?

What do you notice about the way the words are arranged in each poem? Why do you think they are printed that way?

Why is the poem called "Greedy"? Why is the last word printed the way it is?

Think about a topic for a poem and a shape to fit the topic. Write a concrete poem and share it with a friend.

The children will: ☐ interpret to note arrangement and make inferences ☐ write to create a concrete poem

Write the meaning of each cartoon and underline the word that has another meaning.

Write a sentence to show one other meaning for the word you underlined.

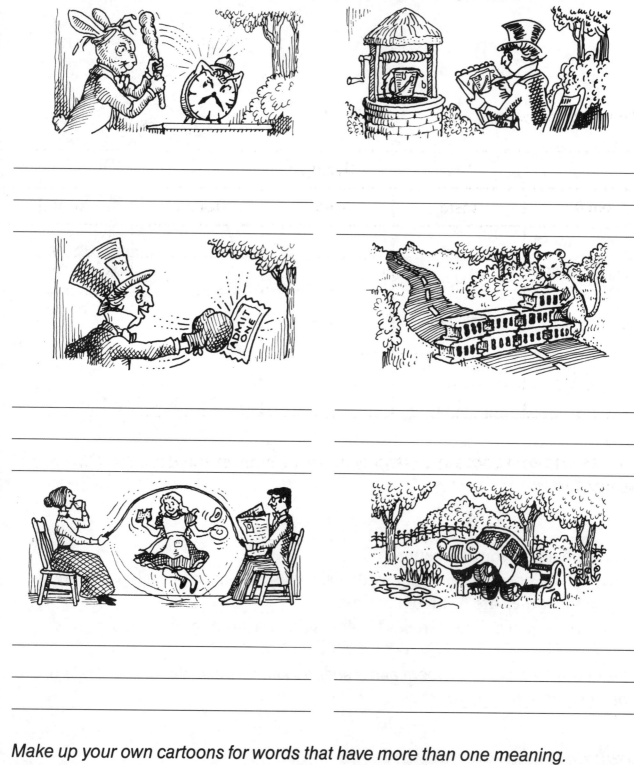

Make up your own cartoons for words that have more than one meaning.

Viewing/Writing

A Mad Tea Party

Complete the chart.

Orange				
smell	**taste**	**sight**	**touch**	**sound**

Choose one item from each category and write a poem about orange. Give your poem a title.

_____

_____

_____

_____

_____

_____

Share your poem with your friends.

A Few More Fables

Read each fable and write a moral for it.

The Dog and His Shadow

Once a Dog found a juicy piece of meat and decided to carry it home to enjoy it. On the way he ran along a log lying across a deep stream. Looking down, he saw his shadow running along the water. He was sure it was another dog carrying an even juicier piece of meat, and he wanted that too. So he snapped at the shadow. But when he did, the piece of meat dropped out of his open mouth into the deep water, and he was left with nothing at all.

The Fox and the Crow

A Fox saw a Crow light on a branch, carrying a large piece of cheese in its beak. Now the Fox loved cheese, so he decided to find a way to get it.

"Good morning, Crow," he said smoothly. "What a fine-looking bird you are! How glossy and black your feathers are! And what bright eyes you have! I'm sure your voice must be just as beautiful as the rest of you. Do sing me a little song!"

The Crow was delighted with these compliments. He opened his mouth and began to caw. Down dropped the cheese and up jumped the Fox. He snapped up the cheese and licked his lips. "That will do, my foolish friend," he said. "All I really wanted was the cheese."

The Lion and the Mouse

One day a Lion was asleep in the woods, and a little Mouse ran across his paws and woke him up. The angry Lion trapped the Mouse under one huge paw and was about to eat him up in one bite. "Please don't eat me, O King of Beasts," squeaked the Mouse. "Let me go just this one time. I promise I'll do you a good turn one day soon."

The Lion roared with laughter. He was so amused at the idea that a tiny little mouse was offering to help him that he raised his paw and let the Mouse escape.

Not long afterwards, the Lion became trapped in a big net that some hunters had set in the wood. The Mouse heard the Lion's unhappy roars and ran to see what was wrong. When he saw the net, he at once began to gnaw through the ropes. Soon the Lion was free. "Now, Your Majesty, wasn't I right?" asked the Mouse.

Discuss the morals you wrote with your friends and talk about other lessons that you could teach through fables.

The children will: ☐ interpret to note main idea ☐ talk to compare and explore ideas

Complete these old sayings with old endings or new ones, or both.

All that glitters is not _____

_____

A bird in the hand is _____

_____

He who hesitates is _____

_____

A stitch in time saves _____

_____

Slow and steady wins _____

_____

Haste makes _____

_____

Many hands make _____

_____

Cheaters never _____

_____

Look before you _____

_____

All work and no play _____

_____

If at first you don't succeed _____

_____

The early bird _____

_____

Share your sayings with your classmates.

The children will: ☐ extend to create endings to proverbs

All About Fables

Complete the chart for fables you have read.

Title	Characters	Description of characters	Moral
The Hare and the Tortoise			
The Fox and the Grapes			
The Dog in the Manger			
The Grasshopper and the Ant			
The Camel Dances			
Other:			

Discuss with a friend or a group of friends how the characters and fables are similar and how they are different.

The children will: ☐ chart to compare fables

Amanda put on her glasses so she wouldn't trip over the mess on her floor, and took out the toothpaste tube. She undid the cap. Slowly, ever so slowly, the purple bubble began to grow. Amanda bristled with impatience. She could just about see the genie inside the bubble. His eyes were tightly closed. He rubbed them, blinked a few times, and yawned.

"It's about time! You took so long I thought I was hibernating! You're supposed to use me every day. Anyone but a little kid would! On the other hand, what do you mean, waking me up so early? I need my sleep, you know!"

Amanda felt so confused she started to apologize, then stopped, since she didn't know what to apologize for.

"Can you make me as neat a writer and drawer as Cynthia?" she asked, and with sudden inspiration added, "Make me all neat. Make my shirts stay tucked in, my socks not wrinkly, and my hair stay combed—and easy to comb too. And how about my bedroom?" She looked at the litter: toys, a half-eaten cookie, clothes on the floor mixed with her bedspread, her bed full of lumps. "Can you make it neat too?"

"No! That's too many wishes. I told you only one. Union rules."

Suddenly Amanda heard footsteps coming down the hall. She threw the genie into the closet, closed the door, and leaned against it.

Her mother opened the bedroom door. "Aren't you dressed yet? It's after eight. And who were you shouting at?"

"No one." Amanda crossed her fingers behind her back. "No person." The genie wasn't really a person, she reasoned. "I was—uh—practising."

Mrs. Atkins didn't look convinced. "Just hurry up now, and by the way, I want this room cleaned up today. It's worse than a pigsty."

"Yes, Mum. I'm working on it now." She leaned hard against the jiggling closet door.

Mrs. Atkins opened the bedroom door more widely. "Don't start it now, Amanda, or you'll be late. Do it after school . . . And why are you rattling the door like that?" She took another step into the room and there was a dreadful noise from the closet as if everything in it had started to dance around.

The pressure on the door was more than Amanda could bear. Just as her mother started across the room Amanda yelled, "The stove! I can hear the timer!"

"Drat, that'll be the eggs. Now get dressed or yours will be cold."

As her mother closed the bedroom door Amanda opened the one to the closet. The purple bubble had grown to an immense size and was frothing. All the toys, books, and games which had teetered precariously on Amanda's shelves were now on the floor. The toothpaste tube had a dent in the bottom.

"Thank you very much," the genie said icily. "How would you like to be unceremoniously chucked into a messy closet like that when you're only trying to do your job?"

"I'm very sorry, but I didn't want my mother to find you."

"She might know how to treat a genie better than you do."

48

"Oh, no, she wouldn't. She'd want to paint you. You'd have to pose. She'd capture your essence."

"My what?"

"Your essence. The real you."

"The real me?"

"That's what she does. She's an artist."

The genie rolled his eyes. "She sounds more dangerous than you!"

"She's not dangerous, she's really nice. But she makes you pose and that's boring. You'd have to sit still . . . and she wouldn't let you go to sleep."

"Not sleep! Well!"

"Now, about my wish," Amanda said, feeling more in control. It was apparent one had to be firm with genies.

"All right, your wish, but be quick." He looked toward the bedroom door as if expecting Mrs. Atkins again.

Amanda's brain had shifted __1__ high gear. "I wish __2__ would make everything about __3__ , including what I do, __4__ . That's only one wish, __5__ it?" She smiled persuasively.

__6__ genie held his pipe __7__ his hand and rubbed __8__ nose. "You are a __9__ one." He frowned. "It's __10__ irregular, but I guess __11__ all right. Just don't __12__ it too often. At __13__ end of the month __14__ have to give a __15__ important report, you know." __16__ disappeared into his tube __17__ amazing speed and Amanda __18__ the orange cap.

Suddenly __19__ in her room began __20__ fly around, bumping and __21__ for position. The pieces __22__ games sorted themselves out __23__ the jigsaw puzzles and __24__ into the right boxes. __25__ boxes flew onto the __26__ . Amanda watched the bed __27__ itself, the dolls walk __28__ to the wall and __29__ up, the dirty clothes __30__ into the laundry hamper __31__ the clean ones into __32__ drawers. In the midst __33__ this her nightgown undid __34__ and flew under the __35__ and her school clothes __36__ its place. It was __37__ the cyclone which had __38__ Dorothy to Oz. Amanda __39__ on to the closet __40__ for fear of being tidied away as well.

Slowly the room quieted. Amanda had never seen it so neat. She had never known it had so much floor space. She had only to empty the wastepaper basket.

"That was fast," Mrs. Atkins said approvingly when Amanda appeared for breakfast. "And don't you look nice. How did you do your hair?"

"I don't know," Amanda replied truthfully. As she sat down at the table she automatically reached up to readjust her glasses, which usually slipped when she bent over. But this time her glasses did not slip. Her hair did not flop onto her plate. Her knife did not fall onto the floor. She was able to put jam on her toast without slopping it on the table and she was able to get the lid back on the jam pot without getting the outside sticky.

Amanda felt neat. She felt so neat she wondered if she had been pasted together. Her socks were snug around her knees and from the tightness of her shoes she knew the laces were still done up. She wondered if she wasn't a bit too neat.

Adapted excerpt from *The Toothpaste Genie* by Frances Duncan, copyright © 1981 by Frances Duncan. By permission of Scholastic-TAB Publications Ltd.

JOURNEYS

Beasts, Birds, Bugs, and Us

1. Look through magazines and cut out pictures of pets and other animals. Arrange the pictures in groups to make a photo display. Ask some friends to add more pictures to the display.

 2. Do you have a favorite animal? What is it that you like about it—its beauty, its fierceness, . . .? Make up a list of favorite animals and your reasons for liking them.
Post your list in the classroom so others can add to it.

 3. Work with a partner to create a wild animal environment such as a woodland, a plain, or a jungle. You could use flour-and-water paste or papier-mâché to make the ground, and find models of the animals that live in your environment or make them out of clay.

 4. Many animals around the world are in danger of dying off and becoming extinct. Find out about one endangered animal and give an oral report about it. Tell why it is in danger and what you think people could be doing to help it. Ask your listeners if they have any other ideas for helping the animal. You could tape-record your report and play it as a radio program or you could present it as a TV program, with pictures, posters, and charts.

 5. Make up an "Animal Pursuits" game. Each person in your group or class could write a few cards with an amazing fact on one side and the animal's name on the other. For example, on one side you could write:

> I am the fastest runner in the animal kingdom. I can run 80 km an hour. Who am I?

On the other side you would write the answer: *Ostrich*.
When you and your friends have played the game enough times to know all the answers, you could make up some new cards!

 6. Find a tape or record of *Carnival of the Animals* by Saint-Saëns and listen to it. Can you hear the lion's roar? Does the music tell you that this is the king of the beasts? Can you tell when the elephant comes in? Which animal's music do you like best? Why? Play the music for a friend and compare your reactions.

The children will: ☐ choose to complete unit activities

7. Imagine you are an animal with a special problem—a porcupine who needs a back rub, or a giraffe with a sore throat. How would you get someone to help you?

Think of some animal problems and invent serious or silly solutions for them. Write and illustrate an *Animal Fix-It* book and put it in the Reading Centre.

8. People use sayings like *hungry as a bear, happy as a lark, . . .* Match each of these words with the animal you think it describes:

greedy	mule
stubborn	cat
sly	fox
timid	ox
stupid	pig
curious	mouse

Find out if these words really fit the animals. Look up the animals in an encyclopedia and share the facts and opinions you find with a partner.

9. Pictures of animals are often used in advertisements. For example, soft fluffy kittens are used to sell toilet paper and facial tissues. What animal would you use to sell a detergent that gets clothes "whiter than white"? jeans that are really tough and sturdy? Think of an animal that you would use to sell a product and make a full-page ad. Create a brand name for your product and a slogan for your ad. Draw or paste a picture of the animal in your advertisement.

10. Find a book in the library about people and animals. Here are some you might enjoy reading.

Andy Bear: A Polar Cub Grows Up at the Zoo, by Ginny Johnston and Judy Cutchins.
Cindy: A Hearing Ear Dog, by Patricia Curtis.
Follow My Leader, by James Garfield.
The Optimists of Nine Elms, by Anthony Simmons.
Seven Feet Four and Growing, by H. Alton Lee.

Read the poem.

Rags

My dog is not a pretty dog
She'll never win a prize.
She looks just like a ragged mop—
It's hard to find her eyes!

Her paws, as big as dinner plates,
Leave mudprints every place,
Her tongue's a long red washcloth
And she slurps it up my face.

Her fur's as shaggy as a bear's
And feels like wire bristle,
Her ears are droopy, floppy flags—
They perk up when I whistle.

She chases cats, she chases cars,
She never will obey.
And yesterday she bit my aunt.
I love her anyway!

— SHARON STEWART

Read the poem again and underline groups of words that create pictures in your mind.

Write each group of words where you think it belongs in the chart on page 5.

The children will: ☐ interpret to identify and classify word pictures   ☐ talk to generate and classify word pictures

as...as	like	is, are

Share your chart with a partner and talk about other words you might use to create similar mind pictures.

Add your mind pictures to the chart.

The children will: ☐ interpret to identify and classify word pictures   ☐ talk to generate and classify word pictures

Pet Words

Write the words that describe the pets in "Best Friends."
Add other words that could describe dogs and cats.

Dogs: _____

_____

_____

_____

_____

Cats: _____

_____

_____

_____

_____

Use the words to complete the chart.

Words to Describe Dogs and Cats		
looks	**feel**	**personality**

Make a chart like this for birds or gerbils or turtles, or any other pet animals.

The children will: ☐ interpret to list descriptive words ☐ chart to classify descriptive words

Read the article and answer the questions.

Have you ever wished you could do something to help animals? You can! The Kindness Club is for children who really care about animals.

The Kindness Club began in 1959. Aida Flemming of Fredericton, New Brunswick, wanted to help stray and mistreated animals. When she couldn't get help from adults, she asked New Brunswick school children to send her essays about animal welfare. She not only received hundreds of essays but also many letters asking if there was a club children could join to help animals. And so The Kindness Club was born.

There are two ways to join The Kindness Club. If you know other children who are interested, you can all become members and start your own branch of the club. Then you all vote on who will be in charge and what projects you want to do. But even if you can't find anyone else, you can still join The Kindness Club as a Lone Raccoon.

All Kindness Club members take this pledge: "I promise to be kind to animals as well as people and to speak and act in defence of all helpless living creatures." Members keep in touch by attending club meetings, reading the club newsletter, and exchanging ideas with pen pals. They learn how to care for pets, read about wild animals, and take field trips. They also carry out projects such as cleaning up litter in parks and wildlife areas and helping to care for animals at local shelters.

Today there are Kindness Club kids in twenty-two countries around the world. If you want to join the club, here is a membership form you can copy and use.

The Kindness Club, 65 Brunswick Street, Fredericton, NB   E3B 1G5

NAME _____ BIRTHDATE _____

                                                day   month   year

ADDRESS _____

_____

                                           postal code

SPECIAL INTERESTS _____

MEMBERSHIP DUES ENCLOSED   ☐ $1.00 under 18....   ☐ $2.00 adult

---

What do members of the club do to help and learn about animals?

What questions would you like to write to the club about?

If you joined the club, what projects to help animals would you like to do?

Share your ideas and answers with your friends.

The children will: ☐ interpret to note information ☐ question to relate to personal experience

A Dog Named Ben

Jot down six important events from "The Foundling."

☐ _____   ☐ _____

☐ _____   ☐ _____

☐ _____   ☐ _____

Number the boxes to show the order of the events.
Use the order and your jot notes to write a summary of the story.

_____

_____

_____

_____

_____

_____

_____

_____

_____

_____

_____

_____

Share your summary with your classmates. Talk about what you think makes a good summary.

The children will: ☐ jot to sequence events and write a story summary

The children will: ☐ web to summarize and plan a personal narrative

Jot down the story ideas.

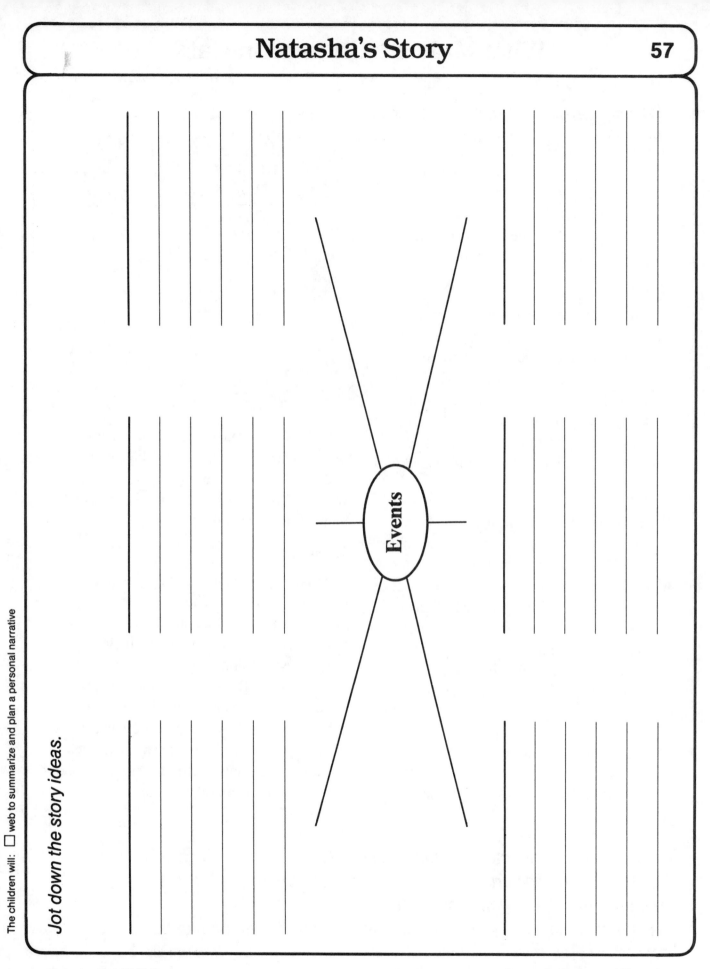

Events

Read the article.

How can a cat-show judge ever decide which animal deserves to be a winner? It's not as difficult as it seems. Only certain breeds of cats are judged, and each cat must match the standards set for its breed. Here are the judging standards for four breeds of cat.

Siamese

Champion Siamese cats are medium in size, with long necks and legs. They have wedge-shaped heads and large, pointed, batlike ears. Their tails are long and tapering. Their short sleek fur is whitish or creamy with darker markings called "points" on the legs, feet, face mask, ears, and tail. Siamese cats' eyes are bright-blue and almond-shaped.

Persian

Prize-winning Persian cats are quite large, with deep chests, short sturdy legs, and short bushy tails. Their fur is long and silky, and forms a thick ruff around the neck and a long frill between the front legs. The fur may be red, black, white, blue, or cream in color. Persians have round massive heads, with small rounded ears and large round eyes. Their eyes may be blue, copper, or green.

Manx

Manx cats have an unusual body shape: they have no tail at all, and they have high rumps because their back legs are longer than their front legs. They have large round heads with broad muzzles. Their eyes are big and round, and are blue or copper in color. Their fur is short and very thick in texture. It comes in many different colors.

Abyssinian

Abyssinians have muscular bodies, slim legs, and small oval paws. Their faces are triangular and their ears are large and pointed. Their long tapering tails are tipped with black. The most unusual thing about Abyssinians is their fur. The short, thick, glossy coat has several bands of color on each hair. This gives the fur a flecked or ticked look. These cats are red or red-brown, with orange fur underneath. Their almond-shaped eyes are hazel, gold, or green, and are rimmed with black.

Skim the article and underline things that judges look for in each breed of cat.
Use the underlined parts to make a web for each breed.
Add any other things you know about.
Use the information in your webs to make a chart of champion cats.

The children will: ☐ skim to identify criteria for judging cats ☐ web to chart information on cat breeds

Bricksie and the Fleas

Complete the chart.

Cause	Effect
_____ _____ _____	Bricksie twitched in his sleep.
Bricksie's hair was thick.	_____ _____ _____
_____ _____ _____	Fleas can crawl easily between hairs.
A flea bit Bricksie.	_____ _____ _____
_____ _____ _____	The Mites gave Bricksie a bath.

What causes can you think of for these effects?
A mouse squeaks.   A chipmunk pops down a hole.

What effects can you think of for these causes?
A cat wants its supper.   A dog wants to go outdoors.

Think of more causes and effects and share them with friends.

The children will: ☐ chart to record causes and effects   ☐ talk to relate cause and effect to personal experience

Reading/Writing/Speaking

Mighty Mites on a Shaggy Dog

Read the tips and discuss them with a partner or your group.

1. Decide who you want to interview. Tell the person why you want to do the interview, get his or her permission to do it, and arrange a time and place when the two of you can meet.

2. Gather background information on the person's work, skills, or hobbies before you do the interview.

3. Decide what things you would like to find out and try to think of questions that will get the kind of information you want.

4. Make up questions that will get more than one-word or one-sentence answers.

5. Write down the questions that are most important to you and take them to the interview. Don't try to ask too many questions.

6. Tape-record the interview if you can—it's easier than trying to write everything down. (Be sure to practise using the tape-recorder before you do the interview.)

7. During the interview, don't be afraid to follow up interesting ideas that come up in the conversation.

8. Don't ask questions that the person has really answered already in answering a previous question.

9. Jot note important points as a backup in case the tape doesn't pick up everything.

10. Remember to thank the person you interviewed. Ask if the person would like to see a final draft of the written interview before it is published anywhere.

Use the ten tips to help you prepare and conduct an interview with someone who is an expert at a job, or hobby, or sport.

The children will: ☐ interpret to identify and talk about interviewing techniques   ☐ interview to obtain information from an expert

Write words that describe each character.

Nicholas				
Mother				
Father				
Tony				

Use the chart to help you answer these questions.

1. How are Nicholas's mother and father alike?

    _____

    _____

2. Why do you think Nicholas and Tony are friends?

    _____

    _____

3. Which word do you think best describes Nicholas? Why?

    _____

    _____

4. Which word do you think best describes his mother? Why?

    _____

    _____

5. Which character do you like best? Why?

    _____

    _____

The children will: ☐ chart to develop characteristics and compare characters

Read the description of Fluffy and think of words that would fit in the blanks.

    We got Fluffy last spring. Some ___1___ brought him to us after a ___2___ killed his mother and brothers and ___3___ . He was so tiny he fit ___4___ into my hand, like a small, ___5___ ball of fuzz. He couldn't eat ___6___ food yet, so we fed him ___7___ milk from a baby bottle.

    After ___8___ while, we started giving Fluffy solid ___9___ like bread and fruit and vegetables, ___10___ meat. We were careful about his ___11___ and tried to give him proper ___12___ for a raccoon. But Fluffy wasn't ___13___ fussy about his diet as we ___14___ . He ate anything he wanted to. ___15___ it didn't take him long to ___16___ out how to get the food ___17___ wanted. One time when we opened ___18___ fridge door we found him sitting ___19___ , munching on a pear! And no ___20___ where we hid the jam, which we used to give him as a treat once in a while, he always found it.

Write a word that would fit and make sense for each blank.

1. _____ 11. _____
2. _____ 12. _____
3. _____ 13. _____
4. _____ 14. _____
5. _____ 15. _____
6. _____ 16. _____
7. _____ 17. _____
8. _____ 18. _____
9. _____ 19. _____
10. _____ 20. _____

Share your words with a partner. Then read the description on pages 45–46 of "A Boy and His Raccoon" to compare the author's words with yours.

The children will: ☐ hypothesize to predict and confirm word choice

Read each group of sentences and try different ways of combining them into one sentence. Write the sentence that you think sounds best.
Share your sentences with a partner.

1. We played in the woods.
   We played every day.
   We played all summer long.

   _____

   _____

2. Fluffy could climb like a monkey.
   Fluffy could walk along a clothesline like an acrobat.

   _____

   _____

3. Fluffy liked to get into his basin.
   He liked to splash water over his head.
   He liked to lick his fur clean.

   _____

   _____

4. We put Fluffy in the cage.
   Fluffy didn't like the cage.

   _____

   _____

5. They left Fluffy in the woods.
   They left him near a swamp.
   They drove away.

   _____

   _____

Look through your writing portfolio. Are there any sentences you could improve by combining them?

The children will: ☐ experiment to combine sentences ☐ edit to combine sentences in personal writing

Read the story.

It had been raining all afternoon. Tara stood by the kitchen window and traced a raindrop as it slid down the outside of the glass. She followed it with her finger till it stopped at the ledge, then looked up for another. That was when she saw the bird. It stood on the clothesline, flapping its wings but not flying. Something was wrong with its feet.

Tara didn't like birds. They squawked in her window and peered at her with beady eyes. Just thinking of their sharp beaks and dry, scratching claws gave her goose pimples.

The rain turned to ice and struck the glass with clattering pellets. Through the frosty pane Tara could see other birds clinging to the line. Beyond, where the clothesline joined the garage, more birds were bathing in the gutter under the roof. The moment they climbed out, dripping wet, onto the line, their feet froze fast to the cord.

One bird after another stuck to the clothesline, like a row of wooden puppets. By now, the first bird had stopped fluttering. Its soggy feathers were slowly turning to ice.

Tara watched in horror. She didn't like the thought of touching birds, but she couldn't just stand by the window and let them freeze. She hesitated, then pulled on her jacket and ran outside to the clothesline stoop. She yanked the line toward her, knocking its icy coating into the pulley. The first brown bird trembled as it looked at her.

"Why, you're more scared than I am. Don't be afraid. I'm going to help you."

Tara cupped one hand over the bird's icy claws. With her other hand, she made a warm cocoon over its body, holding the small, shivering creature until her fingers ached. Finally, she tried to loosen the frozen claws that were wound tightly around the line. The bird struggled feebly. One foot came loose. Then the other. The wings under Tara's hand moved a little.

"You can do it, little bird. Come on! Flap your wings." She pushed gently against the backs of its thighs where pale yellow wing feathers joined the dark body.

"Fly away, little bird!"

The bird fluttered, then flew to a tall spruce tree. Tara rubbed her hands together, warmed them with her breath, and started to work thawing out the feet of the second bird in line. Then the third. Soon all the birds were nestled safely in the spruce tree. Tara knew if any more landed in the gutter, they would skate, not swim. By now even the bristles of grass were like icicles.

Tara tried to warm her frozen hands in the sleeves of her jacket and called out, "Fly away, little birds. And if you come back tomorrow, there'll be food for you."

— MARGARET HIGHAM

Compare "Tara and the Birds" with "The Visitor." Use a chart or diagram to make your comparison.

The children will: ☐ chart or diagram to compare two stories

Read the poem and talk about it with your friends.

Speak gently, Spring, and make no sudden sound;
For in my windy valley, yesterday, I found
Newborn foxes squirming on the ground—
          Speak gently.

Walk softly, March, forbear the bitter blow;
Her feet within a trap, her blood upon the snow,
The four little foxes saw their mother go—
          Walk softly.

Go lightly, Spring, oh, give them no alarm;
When I covered them with boughs to shelter them from harm,
The thin blue foxes suckled at my arm—
          Go lightly.

Step softly, March, with your rampant hurricane;
Nuzzling one another, and whimpering with pain,
The new little foxes are shivering in the rain—
          Step softly.

—LEW SARETT

How is this poem like "The Snare"?

Which poem do you like better? Why?

Why do you think the poets wrote the poems?

Do you think everyone would agree with what the poets are saying?

If people have strong feelings about a topic, do you think it's a good idea for
them to write a poem about it? What else could they do?

"Four Little Foxes," a poem by Lew Sarett, from *Slow Smoke*, copyright 1953 by
Lew Sarett. Used by permission of Lloyd Sarett Stockdale.

Reading/Speaking

The children will: ☐ interpret and talk to compare poems

The Snare

Read the radio program.

ANNOUNCER: This is Bob Baxter with "The Phone-In Show." Today we'll be talking about trapping wild animals. We want to know whether you're for it or against it. Hey, we have our first call. Hello there. What's your opinion about trapping?

CALLER 1: Well, I know some trappers who live up in the Far North, and trapping is the only way they can earn money. They only use traps approved by the government and don't trap more animals than the law allows.

ANNOUNCER: Thank you for your opinion. Now let's hear from our next caller. Hi. Are you for or against trapping?

CALLER 2: Against! Trapping is cruel. Trappers don't always set their traps right, so the animals aren't even killed instantly. Trapping should be made illegal.

ANNOUNCER: So we've heard from people both for and against. Let's see what our third caller has to say.

CALLER 3: I think trapping is necessary. It helps control the numbers of wild animals. The government banned trapping in Algonquin Park a while ago, and guess what happened? The beavers bred in such great numbers that they ran out of food. They ruined a lot of beautiful and valuable trees in the park, and many of them starved to death!

ANNOUNCER: OK. Let's take one more call before our station break. Hello. This is "The Phone-In Show." What do you think about trapping?

CALLER 4: I'm against it. Maybe trapping was all right long ago, but today we don't need furs—we can make warm clothing out of lots of different materials. And I'd like to disagree with the last caller. I think it's better for wild animals to live and die naturally. Even if some beavers starve to death it's better than if they die in traps!

ANNOUNCER: Well, that wraps up the first part of our show. We've had two callers in favor of trapping and two against. What do the rest of you folks out there think?

Discuss these questions, and other questions you think of, with your friends.

What do callers in favor of trapping say?

What do callers against trapping say?

Which arguments are the most persuasive? Why do you think so?

What other arguments for or against trapping can you think of?

The children will: ☐ interpret to identify and evaluate point of view

Jot down information you got from listening to the paragraph and the poem.

Paragraph	Poem
_____	_____
_____	_____
_____	_____
_____	_____
_____	_____
_____	_____
_____	_____

Answer the questions and discuss them with some friends.

1. In what ways is the information the same?

_____

_____

2. In what ways is the information different?

_____

_____

3. How would you compare the way you listened for information in the poem and in the paragraph?

_____

_____

4. Would you rather listen to description in a poem or in a paragraph? Why?

_____

_____

The children will: ☐ attend to list and compare information in two forms ☐ talk to state and justify preferences

Read the information.

Species	Where it lives	Why it's endangered	What's being done
Sea Otter	– North Pacific Ocean	– hunting – pollution in the water	– laws against hunting
Blue Whale	– all the oceans of the world	– hunting – people fish for *krill*, the fish whales eat	– laws against hunting
Giant Panda	– jungles of southern China	– used to be hunted – pandas only eat bamboo and it's scarce	– laws against hunting – finding new foods pandas can eat – breeding in zoos

Find out about other endangered species and add them to the chart. Use the information in the chart to make a poster, a brochure, a tape-recorded news report or commercial, or a mural about endangered animal species.

The children will: ☐ interpret and chart to note and extend information ☐ expand to represent information

1. Think of an animal that's most unlike you. Jot down some differences between the two of you.

Me	**Animal:** _____

2. Write a paragraph that tells how the two of you are different. Tell all about yourself first and then all about the animal.
3. Write another paragraph about the two of you. This time tell about each difference between you, one at a time.
4. Draw a picture that shows the differences.

Share your paragraphs and drawings with your friends.

A Zoo of Things to Do

Choose two or more activities to do, by yourself or with a friend.

1. A group of lions is called a *pride of lions*. What are groups of these animals called?

   a _____ of zebras   a _____ of giraffes

   a _____ of wolves   a _____ of whales

   a _____ of monkeys   a _____ of birds

   a _____ of fish   a _____ of snakes

2. A baby elephant is called a *calf*. What are babies of these animals called?

   seal _____   kangaroo _____   goat _____

   lion _____   horse _____   swan _____

   wolf _____   goose _____   deer _____

3. A lion and lioness are mates. Who is the mate of each of these animals?

   tiger _____   duck _____   vixen _____

   mare _____   bull _____   peahen _____

   ram _____   gander _____   boar _____

4. Koalas eat eucalyptus leaves. What do these animals eat?

   elephants _____   polar bears _____   lions _____

   giraffes _____   whales _____   alligators _____

5. What word would you add that would belong in each group?

   zoo, zoology, _____   nature, native, _____

   danger, endangered, _____   capture, captive, _____

   prison, imprison, _____   survive, survivor, _____

   exhibit, exhibitor, _____   wild, wildebeest, _____

The children will: ☐ choose and experiment to play with words

Late one night something woke me up from a sound sleep. What was it? I lay very still in the darkness, listening, and then it came again; a strange scratching that sounded like giant fingernails scraping against wood. In the silence, the noise seemed impossibly loud, and I began to imagine a huge scary creature trying to claw its way into the cabin. I shivered under the blankets and struggled to come fully awake. Was it inside already?

I listened hard. The scratching sounds were coming from low down on the far wall, by the window, and they seemed to be travelling slowly upward. I stared across the room. A small, dark head rose above the window sill. I sat bolt upright. Something outside was climbing up the cabin wall! I felt for the flashlight on the floor and shone it on the window. Two eyes glowed in the beam of light. A masked face was looking in through the glass. I just had time to notice round, furry ears and a pointed, black, button nose before the face quickly disappeared. There was a loud slithering noise, a muffled thump, then silence.

"What's up?" John called out sleepily.

"Nothing's up," I whispered. "It's down. A raccoon has just fallen off the window ledge!"

We had not seen the raccoon all winter. During the coldest months he would have been curled up somewhere in a warm nest. But lately the weather had become milder, and the raccoon was up and about. I only hoped the flashlight had not frightened him away from the cabin.

I crept to the ___1___ and watched from behind ___2___ curtain. Before long there ___3___ a soft scratching sound, ___4___ the dark furry shape ___5___ up over the pile ___6___ logs stacked on the ___7___. This time the raccoon ___8___ into the darkened cabin ___9___ cautiously, like a guilty __10__ afraid of being caught. __11__ when no bright light __12__ out to frighten him, __13__ crawled along the window __14__ and out onto the __15__ tray that was covered __16__ peanuts and sunflower seeds __17__ the birds.

Running his __18__ sensitive fingers back and __19__ over the tray, Bandit __20__ 5 each seed and nut __21__ touch alone. Indeed, most __22__ the time his bright __23__ were firmly fixed on __24__ cabin or gazing off __25__ space while his paws __26__ the job of finding __27__ . Raccoons are so clever __28__ their fingers that they __29__ have to see their __30__ to find it!

Bandit __31__ a very hungry raccoon, __32__ the birds' food supply __33__ disappeared into his stomach. __34__ tray was empty, but __35__ was far from finished. __36__ up, he saw the __37__ feeder suspended right above __38__ . I had hung a __39__ piece of cheddar cheese __40__ the feeder—the kind that chickadees love—and it dangled down invitingly. Standing tall on his hind feet, Bandit swayed back and forth under the cheese, examining it from all angles. Would he be clever enough to bring it down?

He batted it back and forth, first with one paw, then with the other, just like a boxer in training. But the cheese was firmly attached to the wire and wouldn't come loose. Finally, Bandit reached up as high as he could and fastened all of his long fingers around the cheese. He pulled hard . . . and then even harder, his eyes half-closed with the strain of pulling. Just when it seemed he was going to fail, the cheese suddenly broke apart and came tumbling down. Bandit had his treat at last! I watched him happily eat his prize and then waddle off to his home in the woods.

Our night-time visitor seemed satisfied, but what about the chickadees in the morning? How could I explain that their breakfast had been eaten? I sleepily turned back to bed. I'd have to get up with the birds to refill their feeder, all because of a masked bandit.

Adapted excerpt from "The Night-Time Bandit" by Janet Foster, originally from *Chickadee Magazine*. January 1984. By permission of The Young Naturalist Foundation.

JOURNEYS

Whoopers and Whoppers and Would You Believe It?

1. What if the sun didn't rise one day? Or the rain fell straight up? Or a whole town blew away? Brainstorm some "What if" ideas with some friends. Suggest some crazy solutions for each problem. Then make up a headline and write a news story about one of the situations. Share your story with your friends.

2. Start a Whopper Swapper Club. Think of an exciting event that happened to you. Jot some ways to exaggerate details and make it sound even more fantastic. Make up a tall story.
Hold a club meeting with some friends and swap your whoppers. Your club could collect the whoppers into a "Book of Tall Tales." You and your friends could also put on a talk show for your class and interview each other about your tall adventures.

3. Think about the great qualities and talents that a friend has. Your friend may be too modest to brag, so you could do it for him or her. You could write a poem, or design a magazine cover that shows your friend as "Person of the Year," or . . .

4. Have you heard about the man who walked across the country backward? About the carrot that grew into a radish? Read about some amazing happenings in *Ripley's Believe It or Not.*
Draw a cartoon to illustrate one of the events and write a funny caption for it.

5. The ancient Greeks told stories about many amazing creatures. Choose two of the following creatures and use encyclopedias to find out about them. Then write down what each was like and what it did. Share your findings with some friends.

Harpy	Minotaur	Cerberus
Medusa	Centaur	Cyclops

6. Think up an incredible invention that would make people's lives easier or more enjoyable. Decide what your invention does and how it works. Then design a poster to advertise it. Include a list of directions for operating it.

The children will: ☐ choose to complete unit activities

7. Write down all of the words that come to your mind when you think of superheroes.
Which ones can you group together? Make a chart or web to show how you would group them.

 8. Who is the greatest superhero of all? Work with some friends to collect cartoons and comics and draw pictures for an art display about superheroes. You could include heroes from the past, present, and future. For each illustration, write a list of the hero's deeds and powers.
Invite your classmates to view the display and hold a vote to see who is the most popular superhero of them all.

 9. Find and play recordings of "Casey Jones" and "The Ballad of John Henry," or ask someone to play and sing the songs for you. Listen with some friends and discuss who you think was the greater hero and why.

 10. Find a book in the library about incredibles and impossibles. Here are some you might enjoy reading.

> *Danny Dunn and the Anti-Gravity Paint*, by Jay Williams and Raymond Abrashkin.
> *Mr. Yowder and the Giant Bull Snake*, by Glen Rounds.
> *Mr. Yowder and the Windwagon*, by Glen Rounds.
> *Ripley's Believe It or Not*, by Robert L. Ripley.
> *The Wacky World of Alvin Fernald*, by Clifford Hicks.
> *Weird and Wacky Inventions*, by Jim Murphy.
> *Whoppers: Tall Tales and Other Lies*, by Alvin Schwartz.

The children will: ☐ choose to complete unit activities

Unit Activities

Read the description.

My brother? He's a blubber ball. The kid's so fat that he can't stand on his own two feet. When he rolls, he jiggles like a mound of jello on the move. He's the king of the weepers too. When he doesn't get his own way, he cries oceans. And he's an awful coward — a wimp, a real cream puff. When anything scares him, he howls till the windows rattle. My brother makes a sissie look like Superman!

He's also a dunce. Just imagine, he's so dimwitted that he thinks comic books are for chewing on! He has chomped up a zillion of them. And he sure is a slob at table manners. This kid doesn't eat food, he slurps it. And he wears his food all over him — in his hair, in his ears, everywhere. It's really gross.

If only he were good-looking it might help. But boy, is he ugly! His head is a bald bowling ball. And he's bowlegged too. Still, I keep hoping he might improve. Maybe when he gets to be a year old.

Write exaggerations where they belong.

genius, man no bullet can kill	brilliant, super, stunning	kick a football to Afghanistan

The children will: ☐ chart to list exaggerations

Complete the chart and share it with a friend.

Selection	Whoopers	Whoppers
Who		
I'm the Single Most Wonderful Person I Know		
Pippi Moves into Villa Villekulla		

Use the chart to help you write answers to these questions.
Discuss your answers with a friend.

1. How are whoopers and whoppers alike? How are they different?
2. Which is the biggest whooper? the biggest whopper? Why do you think so?
3. Which selection is most exaggerated? Why do you think so?
4. Which selection do you like best? Why?

I Can Do Anything!

Complete the sentences with your own exaggerated word pictures.
Share them with a friend.

I climb mountains so high that _____

_____

I dive deep underwater and _____

_____

I fly rockets that_____

_____

I live in a palace that _____

_____

I invent machines that _____

_____

I ride horses as wild as _____

_____

I am so sharp-eared that _____

_____

I play in a garden where _____

_____

I go to a school where _____

_____

I make up such wonderful stories that _____

_____

Make up your own exaggerations and share them with your friends.

The children will: ☐ extend to create exaggerated word pictures

Complete the chart and answer the questions.

Whoppers	Weather?	People?	Animals?	Possible true details?	Impossible exaggerations?
Shingling in the Fog					
A Fast Runner					
Frozen Words					
Riding a Fish					
Split Dog					
Mosquitoes on Snowshoes					
The Bear and the Chinook					

1. In what ways are all whoppers alike?
2. What is your favorite whopper? Why?

The children will: ☐ chart to list details and identify elements of a whopper

Read the newspaper items and decide which items could be true and which couldn't be. Jot down why you think so and share your reasons with your friends.

LOCAL PUMPKIN WINS PRIZE

A giant pumpkin with a mass of 278 kg won a blue ribbon at the County Fair. The pumpkin was grown by Mrs. Noreen Orange, a local gardener. The pumpkin measures 3.5 m around. When asked the secret of her success, Mrs. Orange stated that she gave the plant plenty of water and fertilizer, and that she often sang and talked to it. When asked how she would use the giant pumpkin, Mrs. Orange replied that she expects to be baking a lot of pies for the next local bake sale.

SUPER SNORER CAUSES EARTHQUAKE!

The town of Smithville experienced an earthquake last night. The tremors registered 4 on the Richter scale. Residents report hearing "booming sounds" and "loud roaring noises" just before the quake hit. Scientists believe the earthquake was set off by the snoring of Mr. I. N. Hale of 69 Nose Road. Mr. Hale claims he does not snore. Mrs. Hale, who is hard of hearing, supports her husband's statement.

PUMPKIN PERFECT HOME PROSPECT

A giant pumpkin, estimated to have a mass of 1000 kg, offers an exciting prospect for solving the recent housing shortage. Eager home buyers see the pumpkin as an exciting new concept in house design. The interior is bright and spacious and has been fully air-conditioned to keep it cool in summer. The pumpkin was grown by Mr. Peter P. Eater, who promises that similar models will be available next fall.

SNORES SET WORLD RECORD

Mr. C. P. Snort of 11 Schnozzola Drive has just set a world record for the loudest snores ever recorded. During the early hours of yesterday morning, a sound-measuring instrument held half a metre away from Mr. Snort's nose registered his snores at 88 decibels. Mr. Snort is proud of his achievement, and claims that his snoring never disturbs his sleep. He looks forward to seeing his name in the Guinness Book of Records.

Write some news items of your own and share them.

The children will: ☐ interpret to discriminate real and make-believe ☐ jot to justify opinions ☐ write to create news items

Complete the chart to show things that happened in the story.
The first two events and results have been done to get you started.

Events	Results
Children planted jumping beans.	– beans grew, jerked roots out of the ground, and bushes hopped away
Hens are jumping.	– eggs flipped over in frying pan

The children will: ☐ chart to relate events and results

Write your ideas and share them with some friends. Then make up some situations and see what your friends can do with them.

McBroom sends you a giant egg laid by one of the hens on his farm.
List some things you can do with it. Circle your best idea.

_____   _____

_____   _____

McBroom sends you the seeds from one of his giant watermelons.
List things you can do with them. Circle your favorite idea.

_____   _____

_____   _____

A truck dumps a load of ping-pong balls on your front lawn.
Make a list of ways you can get rid of them. Circle your favorite idea.

_____   _____

_____   _____

You find some broken baby carriages in a dump. How could you use the parts to make something?
Draw a picture of what you could make and write what your invention can do.

The children will: ☐ hypothesize and list to find solutions to problems ☐ illustrate to invent a solution ☐ write to describe a solution

Write the missing place names for "Old Paul's work" in the blanks. Then make a list of the deeds Paul did in these places.

James Bay

Lake Huron

Lake Ontario

Gananoque

Niagara River

Lake Erie

Lake Superior

Winnipeg

1.

2.

3.

4.

5.

7.

8.

Digging the St. Lawrence

Draw a vertical line down through the St. Lawrence River to the line under the map to show where you think the digging was finished at the end of each week. Label the three parts of the line: Week 1, Week 2, Week 3.

time line

Use the map and your time line to answer these questions.

1. Did Paul Bunyan begin digging at the east or west end of the

   St. Lawrence River? _____

2. How many kilometres did Babe dig each week? (Use your ruler or a strip of paper and the scale.)

   Week 1 _____   Week 2 _____   Week 3 _____

3. Which town is closest to where the digging ended each week?

   Week 1 _____   Week 2 _____   Week 3 _____

How many days do you think it took after the digging for Paul to get the

money from Billy Pilgrim? _____
Write what you think happened on each day.

Share your answers with a friend.

The children will: ☐ interpret and observe to extend and infer story events

Answer the questions and share your ideas with a friend.

In what ways are Paul Bunyan and Joe Mufferaw alike?

_____

_____

_____

If they were around today, what sorts of things might they be doing?

_____

_____

_____

Think of two or three of your favorite modern superheroes. How are they like Paul Bunyan and Big Joe Mufferaw?

_____

_____

_____

In what ways are they different from Old Paul and Big Joe?

_____

_____

_____

Which do you like best, Paul Bunyan, Big Joe Mufferaw, or a modern superhero? Explain why.

_____

_____

_____

The children will: ☐ talk, write, and assess to compare superheroes

Further Fearsome Critters

Choose one of the critters and write a caption that describes it and explains what it does and how it behaves.
Give your critter a name.

_____

_____

_____

_____

_____

_____

The children will: ☐ observe to note, question, and invent details ☐ choose to write a description

Read the captions and draw the critters. Then make up a critter and draw a picture of it. Write a caption describing your critter. Share your pictures and your caption.

The Brickpecker

These weird birds live in chimneys. They have brush bristles instead of feathers, and long widespread claws to brace themselves against chimney walls. They live on soot they peck from chimney bricks. Transparent gogglelike skin keeps the soot out of their eyes.

The Frillfish

Frillfish are covered with rosy pink fins that resemble long lacy frills. They have mirrors in their tails so they can admire themselves constantly. Frillfish are so vain that when two of them see each other they burst into tears of rage and envy.

The Shovel Shlink

Shlinks are shy, scaly lizard critters that live in holes in the ground. Their front feet are shaped like shovels so they can dig fast. Their hind feet point backward so they can run away fast. When an enemy attacks, they can scoop dirt in its face while backing away.

_____
_____
_____
_____
_____
_____

The children will: ☐ illustrate to represent details ☐ illustrate and write to invent and describe a creature

Creature Features

Check one of the boxes for each animal. If you check Yes *or* No, *write how you know. If you check* Don't Know, *write what you can do to find out.*

Is the animal real?	Yes	No	Don't know
This pachyderm has two horns on its snout and three toes on each foot. Its eyes are on either side of its head. It peers first with one eye then with the other in order to see straight ahead.			
This rare bird has stiltlike legs, a plump body, and a long neck. It stands 3 m tall and has a wingspread of 6 m. Its eyes are sensitive to light, so it spends the day roosting with its head tucked under its wing.			
This flying mammal uses kite-shaped membranes to glide for up to 70 m. It has a head shaped like a greyhound's. Its teeth are like combs, with about twenty comb teeth growing out of each root.			
This rodent has a coarse leathery hide and a long quilled tail. When attacked, it flings poisoned quills at its enemies. It lives on fruit and sleeps hanging upside down in trees.			

The children will: ☐ interpret to discriminate real and make-believe ☐ write to explain or justify conclusions

Read these story beginnings.

Choose one and write the wildest story you can think of.

When I come home at noon, it's always the same boring lunch — soup and a sandwich. Today it was vegetable soup again, and I was feeling really bored, staring into the soup and stirring the alphabet letters around with my spoon. Suddenly, as I stirred, the letters in my soup began to spell out a message. It said, "Don't eat me."
"Why not?" I asked, hardly believing my eyes.
I stirred the soup again, and the letters spelled|a different message.

I have these awful freckles sprinkled all over my nose and cheeks like grains of red pepper. I hate them! Well, yesterday I saw this sign in a store window: "Try Wonder Lotion. Say good-bye to your warts, corns, double chins, and freckles." So I bought a bottle. Last night I smeared the lotion over my face before I went to bed. When I woke up this morning and looked in the bathroom mirror, I saw the most astonishing sight.

Every Saturday is chore day at my house. It means I have to tidy my room, even though I really prefer it messy. Somehow, I just feel more at home in an untidy room. Last Saturday I had just finished putting everything in place, and my room looked extra unfriendly and cold, when I heard this strange rumbling noise. It was coming from the books on my shelf. It grew louder and louder and then suddenly a growly voice thundered...

I love working on my computer. You may not believe this, but it's like a real person to me. I call it Alvin. Well, yesterday afternoon I had just switched on Alvin and was playing Space Patrol when suddenly the screen went blank and a message appeared. It said, "Spsh Mrs Idg Mdnt tmrw." I stared at the screen and began to feel scared — and excited.

You'll be amazed when you hear this. I was giving my cat his usual evening meal of canned cat food when something extraordinary happened. Usually my cat loves his dinner. Well, at least he always eats it. But today he sniffed at the bowl for a second and then turned his back on it. Now, this is the amazing part. He looked at me and spoke. Actually spoke!

Share your story with your classmates.

The children will: ☐ extend to write a tall tale or whopper

Look at these illustrations from the book The Three and Many Wishes of Jason Reid. *Compare them with the illustrations in the story in* Tickle the Sun *and with those you drew.*

Complete the chart on page 19. Share your chart and your answer to the question with a friend.

The children will: ☐ observe to compare three visual interpretations of a story

Jason	Book	Story	My pictures
Face details			
Body details			
Clothing			

Quicksilver	Book	Story	My pictures
Face details			
Body details			
Clothing			

Which interpretation do you like best? Why?

The children will: ☐ chart to record observations

Sister Dinah cooked some goo:
Wasn't cake and wasn't stew
Wasn't brownies, wasn't fudge—
Looked like motor oil sludge.

Felt like jelly, stuck like paste
Tasted like industrial waste.
Smelled like sneakers, stank like drains
Rumbled like six subway trains

And boiled up with a roar like thunder.
Dinah didn't stop to wonder:
With a grin of wicked glee
She just added TNT.

Sad to say, that was a goof—
Dinah really raised the roof!
Mom still blames her for the fright,
Daddy calls her "Dinah-mite."

—SHARON STEWART

Which words in the poem make pictures you can see? Hear? Touch? Smell? Taste?

Choose two word pictures you like best and write other words that would create similar pictures.
Write your own word pictures and share them with some friends.

The children will: ☐ interpret to note and classify word pictures   ☐ extend to create word pictures

Work with a partner to write your own lines to complete the verses.

She sent him to buy her
    A packet of cheese.
But the cat hurried back

_____.

She sent him to buy her
    A gallon of juice.
But the cat reappeared

_____.

She sent him to buy her
    A dinner of beef.
But the cat scampered home

_____.

She sent him to buy her
    A bowl of ice cream.
But the cat skated in

_____.

The fridge was soon bulging,
    And so was the shelf.

_____

_____.

Share your verses with some friends.

The children will: ☐ hypothesize to predict and complete verses to a poem

Which Words?

Read this part of the story and think of words that would fit in the blanks.

"I got a chicken," Arthur said.

" 1 , where is it?" his mother asked.

" 2   left it in the hall," Arthur   3 . "It only cost thirteen cents a   4 ."

"That's very cheap," his mother said. " 5   you sure there's nothing wrong with   6 ? Maybe it isn't fresh."

"It's fresh,"   7   said. "It's alive."

"You brought home   8   live chicken?" His mother was getting   9 .

"It was the only one I   10   find." Arthur started to cry. "I   11   to all the stores, and nobody   12   any turkeys or chickens or ducks,   13   finally I bought this chicken from   14   old man who raises them in   15   apartment."

Arthur's mother was headed for   16   door. "Momma, it's a very big   17 !" Arthur shouted. She opened the door.   18   chicken was standing there, shifting from   19   to foot, blinking.

"CLUCK," it said.   20   mother closed the door and just stood staring at it. She didn't say anything for a long time.

Write a word that would fit and make sense for each blank.

1. _____   11. _____

2. _____   12. _____

3. _____   13. _____

4. _____   14. _____

5. _____   15. _____

6. _____   16. _____

7. _____   17. _____

8. _____   18. _____

9. _____   19. _____

10. _____   20. _____

Share your words with a partner. Then read the passage on page 202 of "Superchicken" to compare the author's words with yours.

The children will: ☐ hypothesize to predict and confirm word choice

Pippi's garden was really lovely. You couldn't say it was well-kept, but there were wonderful grass plots that were never cut, and old rosebushes that were full of white and yellow and pink roses—perhaps not such fine roses, but oh, how sweet they smelled! A good many fruit trees grew there too, and, best of all, several ancient oaks and elms that were excellent for climbing.

The trees in Tommy's and Annika's garden were not very good for climbing, and besides, their mother was always so afraid they would fall and get hurt that they had never climbed much. But now Pippi said, "Suppose we climb up in the big oak tree?"

Tommy jumped down from the gate at once, delighted with the suggestion. Annika was a little hesitant, but when she saw that the trunk had nubbly places to climb on, she too thought it would be fun to try.

A few feet above the ground the oak divided into two branches, and right there was a place just like a little room. Before long all three children were sitting there. Over their heads the oak spread out its crown like a great green roof.

"We could drink coffee here," said Pippi. "I'll skip in and make a little."

Tommy and Annika clapped their hands and shouted, "Bravo!"

In a little while Pippi had the coffee ready. She had made buns the day before. She came and stood under the oak and began to toss up coffee cups. Tommy and Annika caught them. Only sometimes it was the oak that caught them, and so two cups were broken. Pippi ran in to get new ones. Next it was the buns' turn, and for a while the air was full of flying buns. At least they didn't break. At last Pippi climbed up with the coffee pot in one hand. She had cream in a little bottle in her pocket, and sugar in a little box.

Tommy and Annika thought coffee had never tasted so good before. They were not allowed to drink it every day—only when they were at a party. And now they were at a party. Annika spilled a little coffee in her lap. First it was warm and wet, and then it was cold and wet, but that didn't matter to her.

When they had finished, Pippi threw the cups down on the grass. "I want to see how strong the china they make these days is," she said. Strangely enough, one cup and three saucers held together, and only the spout of the coffee pot broke off.

Presently Pippi decided to climb a little higher.

"Can you beat this?" she cried suddenly. "The tree is hollow."

There in the trunk __1__ a big hole, which __2__ leaves had hidden from __3__ children's sight.

"Oh, may __4__ climb up and look __5__ ?" called Tommy. But there __6__ no answer.

"Pippi, where __7__ you?" he cried, worried.

__8__ they heard Pippi's voice, __9__ from above but from __10__ down below. It sounded __11__ if it came from __12__ the ground.

"I'm inside __13__ tree. It is hollow __14__ down to the ground. __15__ I peek out through __16__ little crack I can __17__ the coffee pot outside __18__ the grass."

"Oh, how __19__ you get up again?" __20__ Annika.

The children will: ☐ hypothesize to predict and confirm word choice

"I'm never coming   21 ," said Pippi. "I'm going   22   stay here until I   23   and get a pension.   24   you'll have to throw   25   food down through that   26   up there. Five or   27   times a day."

Annika   28   to cry.

"Why be   29 ? Why complain?" said Pippi. " 30   come down here too,   31   then we can play   32   we are pining away   33   a dungeon."

"Never in   34   world!" said Annika, and   35   be on the safe   36   she climbed right down   37   of the tree.

"Annika,   38   can see you through   39   crack," cried Pippi. "Don't   40   on the coffee pot; it's an old well-mannered coffee pot that never did anyone any harm. It can't help it that it doesn't have a spout any longer."

Annika went up to the tree trunk, and through a little crack she saw the very tip of Pippi's finger. This comforted her a good deal, but she was still worried.

"Pippi, can't you really get up?" she asked.

Pippi's finger disappeared, and in less than a minute her face popped out of the hole up in the tree.

"Maybe I can if I try very hard," she said and parted the foliage with her hands.

"If it's as easy as all that to get up," said Tommy, who was still up in the tree, "then I want to come down and pine away a little too."

"Wait," said Pippi, "I think we'll get a ladder."

She crawled out of the hole and hurried down the tree. Then she ran after a ladder, pushed it up the tree, and let it down into the hole.

Tommy was wild to go down. It was difficult to climb to the hole, because it was so high up, but Tommy was brave. And he wasn't afraid to climb down into the dark hollow in the trunk. Annika watched him disappear and wondered if she would ever see him again. She peeked in through the crack.

"Annika," came Tommy's voice. "You can't imagine how wonderful it is here. You must come in too. It isn't the least bit dangerous when you have a ladder to climb on. If you only do it once, you'll never want to do anything else."

"Are you sure?" asked Annika.

"Absolutely," said Tommy.

With trembling legs Annika climbed up in the tree again, and Pippi helped her with the last hard bit. She drew back a little when she saw how dark it was in the tree trunk, but Pippi held her hand and kept encouraging her.

"Don't be scared, Annika," she heard Tommy say from down below. "Now I can see your legs, and I'll certainly catch you if you fall."

But Annika didn't fall. She reached Tommy safely, and a moment later Pippi followed.

"Isn't it grand here?" said Tommy.

And Annika had to admit that it was.

JOURNEYS

The Hoboken Chicken Emergency

Could Dracula Live in Woodford?

Predicting As I Read

At the end of...	What I think will happen	What did happen
Chapter 1		
Chapter 4		
Chapter 10		
Chapter 16		
Chapter 19		

The children will: ☐ hypothesize to predict events and outcomes

Could Dracula Live in Woodford?

At the end of...	What I think will happen	What did happen
Chapter 1		
Chapter 4		
Chapter 7		
Chapter 11		

The children will: ☐ hypothesize to predict events and outcomes

Characters in the Novel

Character	Appearance	Personality	My comments

Could Dracula Live in Woodford?
The Hoboken Chicken Emergency

The children will: ☐ jot and chart to identify and describe novel characters

Character	Appearance	Personality	My comments

The children will: ☐ jot and chart to identify and describe novel characters

Reading/Writing

Could Dracula Live in Woodford?
The Hoboken Chicken Emergency

Chapters 1–4

To talk about:

1. In what ways were Jennie and Sam alike at the beginning of the novel? How were they different?
2. Why did Jennie feel that life wasn't fair? How do you think she should deal with her problem?
3. What reasons did Jennie give for thinking that Mr. McIver was a criminal? Do you think her reasons are good ones? Why or why not?
4. How do you feel about one of the main characters being a dog who thinks like a person?
5. What do you think the author's purpose was in the first four chapters?

To do:

1. Work with a partner to list the places Jennie showed Sam on their walks through Woodford. Then draw a map of Woodford showing where the places might be. Compare your map with another pair's.
2. List things you would tell Jennie to do to help her not to be bored.
3. Make a chart that shows the ways Jennie and Sam are alike and the ways that they are different. Add to the chart as you read and talk about more of the book.
4. Reread the description of Mr. McIver's house on page 23. Try to see the house in your mind, then draw it. Compare your drawing with a friend's.

The children will: ☐ talk to explain and clarify opinions and viewpoints ☐ choose to complete activities

Chapters 5–10

To talk about:

1. Were you *surprised* that Jennie could hear Sam's thoughts? Why do you suppose the author did that? And why do you think Jennie can hear Sam but Joan and Beth can't?

2. How are Jennie and Beth alike? How are they different? Do you think Jennie, Beth, and Sam work well as a group? Why do you think so?

3. Why do you think the author ended Chapters 9 and 10 the way she did? Why did she have Jennie and Beth leave coats and shoes behind?

4. Did you agree with Sam that Jennie's and Beth's first list of "How to Investigate a Mystery" was dumb? What do you think of the second list? What would you add? What would you drop?

5. What was the most frightening part of the night's adventure at McIver's house? Why do you think so?

6. What were the most important events in these chapters? Why do you think so?

To do:

1. Create your own list of "How to Investigate a Mystery." Share it with a friend. Compare to see how the lists are the same and how they are different.

2. Prepare a talk about what someone your age should eat to be healthy.

3. Choose the part that you found the most frightening. Read it aloud to a friend, using your voice to show the feelings and suspense.

4. Find out what sheepdogs should eat for a balanced and healthy diet.

5. Work with friends and act out the scene when Sam meets the twins.

6. Make a list of the things in the novel that you think are unbelievable. Keep adding to your list as you reread the novel. Share your list with a friend.

The children will: ☐ talk to explain and clarify opinions and viewpoints ☐ choose to complete activities

Chapters 11–16

To talk about:

1. In what ways does Sam behave like a person? Why does the author have her behave that way?
2. What reasons do Jennie and Beth have for thinking McIver is a vampire? Do you think their reasons are good ones? Why or why not?
3. Do you agree with Jennie that she and Beth had to lie? Have you ever felt lousy because you had to lie about an adventure you had? Why did you feel lousy?
4. Do you think that Sam's adventure alone at McIver's house is necessary to the story? Why do you think the author included it?
5. Jennie said Sam did a lousy job of telling what happened at McIver's house. Sam said she did a great job. What do you think? Why?
6. Why was Noel suspicious when Jennie offered to help him with his deliveries? Are your brothers or sisters ever suspicious when you offer to do them a favor?
7. What gave Jennie and Beth the courage to make the delivery to McIver to rescue Sam? Would you have done it?
8. What details did the author include to add suspense when Jennie, Sam, and Beth are at McIver's house?

To do:

1. Jot in your journal the information you learned about vampires. Then look in a reference book to find out any other facts you could add.
2. Mime Sam's behavior and movements while she was in Mr. McIver's basement.
3. Jennie chews her fingernails when she's nervous. Sam eats. Work with a friend to make a web of things people do when they feel nervous or scared.
4. Draw a map that shows the route Sam took from her house to McIver's and back home. Mark places on the route where something happened and jot or draw the events.

Chapters 17–19

To talk about:

1. How did Jennie and Beth find out that vampires don't really exist? How did they feel when they found out? Were you surprised or did you know all along?
2. Would you like to have Noel for a brother? Why or why not?
3. When Jennie and Beth found out that McIver was a recluse, why didn't they just accept it the way Noel did?
4. Where do you think Jennie and Beth get all their information about criminals and how they behave?
5. Why didn't Jennie and Beth tell McIver the truth?

To do:

1. Make a chart of the qualities you look for in a friend. Then look at your chart to see which of these qualities your friends have.
2. Imagine that McIver can hear Sam, the way Jennie does. Write a dialogue between the two in which Sam explains why she and the girls were spying on him.
3. McIver's house was spooky. Draw a picture of a place that you think looks mysterious or spooky.
4. Write a list of questions that you would have asked McIver in an interview.
5. Write a description of a room in your house so that a blind person could feel what's in it.

The children will: ☐ talk to explain and clarify opinions and viewpoints ☐ choose to complete activities

Chapters 20–21

To talk about:

1. How did the author make this a funny novel? How did she make the mystery scary?
2. Was the ending satisfying? Why or why not?
3. Did your feelings about any characters change as you read the novel? How?
4. If you were writing a sequel to this novel called *Could Frankenstein Live in Woodford?* which characters in this novel would you keep? Which would you drop? What characters might you add?
5. If you could talk to the author, what would you tell her about the novel?

To do:

1. Work with some friends to act out the scene when Sam meets Sheila and Lisa.
2. Write a solution for Sam's problem of having to stay indoors all day.
3. Sam found that Frankenstein was living in Woodford. List some other people or creatures that Sam might find after Frankenstein.
4. Illustrate your favorite scene from this section.

The children will: ☐ talk to explain and clarify opinions and viewpoints   ☐ choose to complete activities

Chapters 1–4

To talk about:

1. What is your favorite funny part in these chapters? Why?
2. Why did Poppa want his family to eat turkey for Thanksgiving even if they didn't like it much? Does his reason make sense? Why or why not? Are there holidays in your family where you eat food you don't like? What are the reasons?
3. Why do you suppose Arthur took Professor Mazzocchi's superchicken? What would you have done? Why?
4. What do you think of the family's reaction to the superchicken?
5. What methods did Arthur use to train Henrietta? Do you think these methods would work with any pet? Explain why you think so.
6. Why did it take so long before the police and firefighters paid attention to what Arthur was saying?
7. Why did Arthur have to take Henrietta back? Do you agree with Arthur's point of view that it wasn't fair?
8. What do you think of Professor Mazzocchi's experiments? Why?

To do:

1. List in your journal the special things you eat and do to celebrate Thanksgiving.
2. Tell or write about an experience you have had in training a pet.
3. Work with a partner and mime or role-play a favorite scene from these chapters.
4. Draw or make a model of one of Professor Mazzocchi's animal experiments. Share your drawings or models with the class.
5. Begin a chart of believable and unbelievable characters and events in the first four chapters of the novel. Compare charts with a friend.
   Keep adding to your chart as you go on rereading the novel.
6. Write directions for "How to Grow a Superchicken," pretending you are Professor Mazzocchi.

The children will: ☐ talk to explain and clarify opinions and viewpoints ☐ choose to complete activities

Chapters 5–7

To talk about:

1. Do you feel that the story has turned kind of sad and yet is still funny? What does the author do to make you feel that way?
2. Why did Professor Mazzocchi leave town after Henrietta escaped? Do you agree that it was more important for him to save his experiments than to take care of Henrietta?
3. Do you agree with the professor that people are sometimes afraid of things they've never seen before and that when they are afraid they do foolish things?
4. Do you think Arthur did a good job of looking for Henrietta? What would you have done if you were Arthur?
5. Arthur did some things he knew his parents wouldn't like. Do you think he was right to do them? Why or why not?
6. Why do you think the author exaggerated the news reports about Henrietta? What examples can you think of when news reports have been exaggerated?
7. The newspapers had printed a picture of Arthur with Henrietta. Why didn't people figure the giant chicken was Henrietta instead of panicking?

To do:

1. Draw a picture of Arthur's dream about Henrietta.
2. In Chapter 6 the author mentions many places and things in Hoboken. Make a list of them. Then choose one of them and illustrate it.
3. Tape-record the radio report about Henrietta being loose in Hoboken.
4. Work with some friends to act out the teachers' meeting when they decided to close the school.
5. Write some headlines that newspapers might have printed about the chicken crisis in Hoboken.
6. Write a summary of these chapters from Henrietta's point of view.

The children will: ☐ talk to explain and clarify opinions and viewpoints   ☐ choose to complete activities

Chapters 8–11

To talk about:

1. How did being hunted affect Henrietta's behavior? Why do you think she behaved the way she did?
2. What do you think of the way the police, the fire department, and other officials behaved?
3. Why do you think television stations and newspapers stopped reporting chicken stories? Why do you suppose people went back to work and school even though the giant chicken was still loose?
4. Do you think the author is making fun of the mayor and the city council? What makes you think so? Why do you think he's doing it?
5. How did Anthony DePalma get the city council to agree to his demands? Do you approve of his methods? Why or why not? If you were mayor or a member of the city council, what would you have done? Why?
6. Anthony DePalma was a very clever man. What proofs can you find for this statement?
7. Were you surprised that the chickenoid trap didn't work? Why or why not?

To do:

1. What if the mayor of Hoboken had written an advertisement for someone to capture Henrietta? Write the advertisement he might have used. The advertisement could describe the job, give the qualifications the person should have, and tell the money that will be paid.
2. Anthony DePalma's slogan was "I snatch for scratch." Think of something that you do well. Make up a slogan to describe it. You might wish to write your slogan on a circular piece of paper and wear it as a button.
3. Make a model of the chickenoid trap that Anthony DePalma used to try to trap Henrietta. Or make a model of a trap you would have used to capture her.
4. Be the television news reporter and read aloud the news reports about Henrietta, or interview DePalma, the mayor, the police chief, and other officials.
5. Reread the description of Anthony DePalma and then illustrate him.

The children will: ☐ talk to explain and clarify opinions and viewpoints ☐ choose to complete activities

Chapters 12–14

To talk about:

1. Why didn't Dr. Hsu Ting Feng want the mayor to ask questions about where Henrietta had come from in the first place?
2. How did Dr. Hsu Ting Feng explain Henrietta's behavior? Do you think his explanation is reasonable? Why or why not? Do you think it's true for people as well as chickens?
3. Why do you think the "Love-Henrietta" campaign worked? Do you think you can change people's attitudes so quickly and easily?
4. What are your favorite examples of the way the author uses exaggeration to make his story funny?
5. What other "tricks" does the author use to make the story funny?
6. Do you think this is a funny novel about a boy and his pet chicken or a novel that pokes fun at people and the way they behave?

To do:

1. Work with a partner. Act out the scene in which Dr. Hsu Ting Feng tells the mayor that Henrietta is like a person.
2. Reread the paragraph on p. 81. Try to figure out how to play fleegle. When you have an idea, work with a friend or friends to play it.
3. Mime how you think Arthur would teach Henrietta to roller-skate.
4. Jot ideas for other tricks that Arthur might teach Henrietta.
5. Web the ways that were used in the publicity campaign to change people's attitude toward Henrietta.

Love-Henrietta Campaign

6. Use the summaries you have made to write this story from the point of view of Henrietta.
7. If Henrietta could talk what might she have said when the mayor gave her the chicken licence? Prepare a speech she might make.

The children will: ☐ talk to explain and clarify opinions and viewpoints   ☐ choose to complete activities

Which Words?

Read the passage.

Jennie went along the fence toward the highway and the front of McIver's house. Turning the corner, she __1__ down the long driveway. ____ a deep breath, she __3__ toward the house. She __4__ see Beth waving from __5__ hiding place. Not yet, __6__. Wait until I get to the door, she thought. __7__ walked up the front __8__ ; her heart thumped and __9__ hands shook. She reached __10__ and knocked. Out of __11__ corner of her eye, __12__ saw Beth cross the __13__ , dragging the board. She __14__ again, harder.

"Wait a __15__ . Hold your horses and __16__ a minute," came a __17__ voice.

From inside the __18__ came the same sounds __19__ had heard before. Click . . . click . . . click . . .

Write a word that makes sense for each blank.

1. _____
2. _____
3. _____
4. _____
5. _____
6. _____
7. _____
8. _____
9. _____
10. _____

11. _____
12. _____
13. _____
14. _____
15. _____
16. _____
17. _____
18. _____
19. _____

Share your words with a partner. Then read the passage on page 130 of Could Dracula Live in Woodford? *to compare the author's words with yours.*

Which Words?

Read the passage.

Arthur got up early __1__ day after Thanksgiving to __2__ Henrietta for a walk. __3__ going out, Arthur made __4__ cup of instant cocoa __5__ himself and gave Henrietta __6__ leftover mashed potatoes. It __7__ just getting to be __8__ when he led Henrietta __9__ into the street. She __10__ blinking. Arthur thought that __11__ might enjoy a walk __12__ the river. They started __13__ east on Fourth Street. __14__ wasn't a single person __15__ the street—it was __16__ early. An empty bus __17__ headed down Washington Street. __18__ driver saw Henrietta and __19__ into a garbage can. __20__ was one of those __21__ ones. It got a __22__ bent, but the bus __23__ damaged. There was a __24__ wind ruffling Henrietta's feathers. __25__ zipped up his jacket.

Write a word that makes sense for each blank.

1. _____
2. _____
3. _____
4. _____
5. _____
6. _____
7. _____
8. _____
9. _____
10. _____
11. _____
12. _____
13. _____

14. _____
15. _____
16. _____
17. _____
18. _____
19. _____
20. _____
21. _____
22. _____
23. _____
24. _____
25. _____

Share your words with a partner. Then read the passage on pages 12–13 of The Hoboken Chicken Emergency *to compare the author's words with yours.*

The children will: ☐ hypothesize to predict and confirm word choice

Weather or Not

1. How can you find out which way the wind is blowing? Make a weather vane or weather sock, using information from science books, and put it in your schoolyard. Check the wind direction in the morning and afternoon for a week. Record your information in a chart and share it with your classmates.

 2. Where would you like to go for a summer or winter holiday? Choose a real place, or make up an imaginary one, and design a travel folder to advertise vacations there. Draw or find pictures to show what the place looks like and describe the kinds of things people can do there.

3. Research, with a partner, some weather "records" for your community. What are the hottest and coldest temperatures ever recorded? The greatest rainfalls and snowfalls? What did people in your community do during those record-breaking days? Write a *Weather Record* book and put it in the Reading Centre.

 4. Brainstorm games or sports that are played during each of the four seasons. Make a web to organize your information and illustrate it with pictures from magazines.

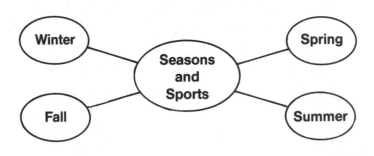

5. Play a tape or record of "Cloudburst" from the *Grand Canyon Suite* by Grofe. Can you hear the storm—howling winds, the thunder and rain? Write a poem to go with the music. Play the music and read your poem for some friends.

The children will: ☐ choose to complete unit activities

6. Read the fable titled "The Wind and the Sun" by Aesop. Work with some friends to act out the fable for your classmates.

7. What would you like to know about hurricanes or tornadoes? With a partner, write down the questions you have and find the answers through research. Share your questions and answers with some classmates.

8. Different clouds bring different weather. Work with a couple of friends to find out about cumulus, cirrus, and stratus clouds. Draw or find pictures of the clouds and give a talk to your classmates, explaining what weather each kind of cloud brings.

9. Imagine you are a weather person for a radio station. Think of some unusual things that could happen to the weather, such as a rainstorm of real cats and dogs or snow in the middle of summer. Prepare your weather reports and present them to some friends or tape record them.

10. Find a book in the library about people and weather. Here are some you might enjoy reading.

> *Gretzky! Gretzky! Gretzky!,* by Meguido Zola.
> *McBroom and the Big Wind,* by Sid Fleischman.
> *Peewee,* by Suzanne Martel.
> *Storm Island,* by Jean MacKenzie.
> *The Long Winter,* by Laura Ingalls Wilder.
> *The Wizard of Oz,* by L. Frank Baum.

The children will: □ choose to complete unit activities

I Didn't Know That!

Reread the article and answer the questions.

1. What facts did you learn that you didn't know before?

   _____

   _____

   _____

2. What were the most interesting facts you read?

   _____

   _____

   _____

3. Which facts did you find the most incredible?

   _____

   _____

   _____

Fact or Fiction?

Here is some more "Wow Weather" information. Research each statement and write if each is fact or fiction. Share your findings with a friend.

1. Thunderstorms turn milk sour.   _____

2. Lightning fertilizes soil.   _____

3. Humidity makes hair curly.   _____

4. Don't take a bath during a
   thunderstorm.   _____

5. Tornadoes happen only on land.   _____

The children will: ☐ reread to explain and formulate opinions   ☐ extend to research information

Jot down ideas in the left column. Write your answers in the right column.

1. Why had Aunt Em and Uncle Henry become gray?

_____   _____

_____   _____

_____   _____

_____   _____

2. What color would you choose to describe Dorothy? Why?

_____   _____

_____   _____

_____   _____

_____   _____

3. Do you think Dorothy will become gray? Why or why not?

_____   _____

_____   _____

_____   _____

_____   _____

4. What color are you? Why do you think so?

_____   _____

_____   _____

_____   _____

_____   _____

The children will: ☐ jot and arrange to organize answers

Look at each picture and write your observations underneath.

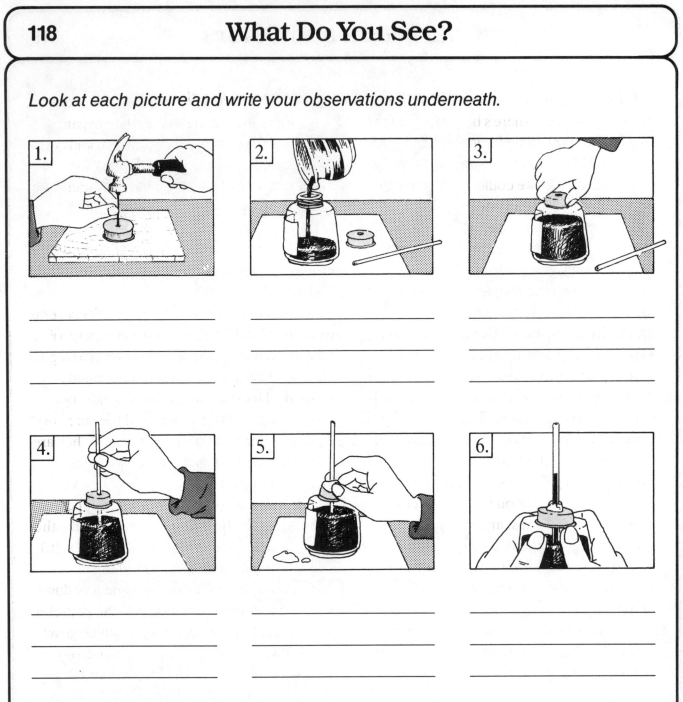

Share your observations with a friend.

What do you think would happen if there was less liquid in the bottle? If there was more liquid?

What do you think would happen if the bottle was in a very hot room?

What conclusion can you make from this experiment?

Discuss your ideas with some friends.

The children will: ☐ observe to note information   ☐ talk to infer information and draw conclusions

Imagine a farmer's field with crops that are drying up because there's been no rain for weeks. Or a spreading forest fire and no rain predicted in the weather forecast. Wouldn't it be wonderful if we could make rain when we needed it? We can—with special "supercooled" clouds and special "seeds" that grow raindrops.

Most clouds are made up of tiny water droplets. When the droplets get too big and too heavy to float in the air, they fall to earth as raindrops. How does this happen? In **supercooled clouds** it happens this way.

In supercooled clouds, water droplets do not freeze, even when the temperature falls below the freezing point, 0°C. But when the temperature falls below -25°C, supercooled water droplets attach to dust specks and freeze, forming ice crystals. As more and more droplets freeze on the ice crystals, they grow into snowflakes, and when the snowflakes grow heavy enough they begin to fall. As they get closer to earth, where the air is warmer, the snowflakes melt—and fall as raindrops.

That's the way rain falls naturally from supercooled clouds: water droplets + dust specks → ice crystals → snowflakes → raindrops.

Weather scientists found out how supercooled clouds make rain from experiments they did in 1946. But they realized that drying crops and burning forests can't wait for natural rain. So they began experimenting to find things that would act the way dust specks did—as "seeds" for forming ice crystals—even if the temperature of supercooled clouds was *above* -25°C. They tried dry ice pellets, sea salt, soil dust, smoke from factory chimneys, and other things, but what worked best was silver iodide.

Silver iodide particles work best for several reasons. They form ice crystals in supercooled clouds even when the temperature is as high as -2°C. They can be sprayed into clouds from airplanes or carried up by wind from smoke pots on the ground. And they are easy to handle and spread widely because they are incredibly tiny. (If each of the 25 million people in Canada were given 80 000 silver iodide particles, and if they each dropped their 80 000 particles into a common pile, the pile would only be the size of a grain of salt.)

Silver iodide particles seeded in supercooled clouds work the same way dust specks do. Water drops attach to the particles and freeze, forming ice crystals, which grow into snowflakes which melt into raindrops when they fall down to warm air near the earth. The important difference is that they can be seeded in supercooled clouds with temperatures as high as -2°C, so they make rain when it's needed.

Make a summary of the article in a chart that compares natural and artificial rainmaking in supercooled clouds.

The children will: ☐ chart to summarize and compare information

True or False?

Decide if each statement is true or false. Then reread "Questions and Answers about Weather" to check your answers.

1. Warm air pulling cooler air causes wind. _____

2. Water vapor is a different form of water. _____

3. Fog, clouds, and smog are all made of water vapor. _____

4. Wind in clouds makes the water droplets move around. _____

5. Sleet and hailstones are frozen raindrops. _____

6. Thunder and lightning do not happen at the same time. _____

Rewrite the false statements to make them true.

_____

_____

_____

_____

_____

Make up your own true and false statements from the article to challenge your friends.

The children will: □ evaluate to interpret statements □ write to make false statements true □ expand to make up true and false statements

Look at the diagram with a partner and read the information about weather satellites.

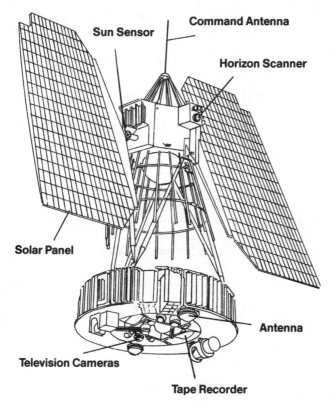

Sun Sensor
Command Antenna
Horizon Scanner
Solar Panel
Television Cameras
Tape Recorder
Antenna

Here's how parts of a weather satellite work.

The sun sensor keeps the solar panels facing the sun. That's important, because cells in the solar panels turn sunlight into electricity, to run the instruments.

The horizon scanner keeps the television cameras aimed at Earth as the satellite orbits. The cameras take pictures and send the picture signals to the tape recorder, where they are stored.

As the satellite passes over a weather station, the antenna beams the picture signals (and other information about temperature, wind, and moisture) down to antennas on earth. Electronic equipment at the station sorts out the signals and makes a copy of the picture.

The command antenna receives instructions from meteorologists at a weather station, telling it what information to collect, record, and send down to Earth.

The next time you watch a weather report on TV, look at the satellite photograph carefully and listen to the forecaster's explanation of what it shows. If you watch every day for a week, you can see and learn how the weather picture changes.

Have you ever seen photographs of the Earth in weather reports on TV? The photos are taken by satellites orbiting around the Earth. Cameras, recorders, and other instruments in the satellite collect information about clouds, temperatures, winds, and moisture in the air, and send it to weather stations on Earth. Meteorologists use this information to make weather forecasts.

Discuss these questions with your partner.
Share your ideas with other classmates.

How are satellites used to make forecasts?
What does each part of a satellite do?
How do you suppose meteorologists made forecasts before satellites?
Why are satellites a meteorologist's best friend?

Weather Signs in Nature

Complete the chart with information you got from listening to the article.

Who, What	Sign	What It Means
Groundhog		

Share your chart with your classmates.

The children will: ☐ attend to obtain information ☐ chart to summarize information

Play the game with some friends.

Give a synonym and an opposite for <u>swiftly</u>	Spell another word that sounds like <u>weather</u>	Give 2 opposites for <u>freeze</u>	Give a synonym and an opposite for <u>rises</u>
Make 2 compound words from any part of <u>thunderhead</u>			Give 2 synonyms for <u>sign</u>
Give 2 synonyms for <u>amazing</u>	**How to play** 1. Start in any square. 2. Roll the die and move clockwise. 3. Answer the question in your square. Score one point for every correct answer. 4. Total the points after each player has had 5 turns. The player with the most points is the winner.		Spell another word that sounds like <u>foul</u>
Give a synonym and an opposite for <u>reliable</u>			Make 2 compound words from any part of <u>snowstorm</u>
Make 2 compound words from any part of <u>sunset</u>			Make 2 compound words from any part of <u>nowhere</u>
Give a synonym and an opposite for <u>drenched</u>	Spell another word that sounds like <u>forth</u>	Make 2 compound words from any part of <u>campfire</u>	Give 2 synonyms for <u>prediction</u>

Think of other words to place in the game squares.
Play the new game with some friends.

The children will: ☐ expand to play a word game

Funny Forecasts

Complete the chart and share it with a friend.

Weather Report	Usual Completions	Author's Completions	My Completions
Cloudy with a chance of _____ _____			
_____ blew in from the northwest			
wind shifted to the east and brought in _____			
_____ becoming heavy at times with occasional _____			
_____ followed by gradual clearing and a _____ in the west			

Reading/Writing/Speaking

Cloudy with a Chance of Meatballs

The children will: ☐ jot to complete a chart

Read the paragraph and write possible describing words for each blank.

There had been three days of sub-zero temperatures after a slight thaw and there was a __1__ crust on the snow. Her snowboots crunched upon it as she skirted the two __2__ oaks beside the house and traced a path across the top of the pasture. She watched her shadow, a __3__, gray companion gliding along beside her in the moonlight. Up ahead the __4__ shapes of the stumps in Mr. Martin's fence looked like witches, their hands outflung across the snow. She sat on a log for a long moment, in the lee of Huron Hill.

Excerpt from *Samantha's Secret Room* by Lyn Cook © 1963. Reprinted by permission of Macmillan of Canada, A Division of Canada Publishing Corporation.

1 _____

2 _____

3 _____

4 _____

Circle the word in each list that you like the best. Then share your choices with a friend and talk about why you think the words you circled are the best.

Brainstorm as many describing words as possible for these words in the paragraph — path, moonlight, snow, log.
Choose the one that you think creates the best picture and illustrate it.

Look at the pictures with a partner and read the description of each place.

Temperatures that fall below -73°C. Seas frozen solid. Gales gusting to hundreds of kilometres an hour. That's winter in Antarctica, the coldest region on earth.

Who would want to live in such a place? Scientists! They come from many countries to do research, living and working in stations dug deep into the ice and snow.

Even in Antarctica, though, summer does come. Cormorants wheel and cry about the cliffs, seals bark and sunbathe on the shore, and hordes of penguins, like headwaiters dressed for dinner, march solemnly to and from the water. Whales spout and dive as they pursue tiny shrimp-like krill, and porpoises and dolphins frolic as they feast on squid.

It's a lively time for people, too, as ships and planes arrive carrying mail, visitors, and fresh supplies. For people and animals alike, Antarctica's summer is a time to celebrate.

Imagine an oasis in the world's largest desert, the Sahara. All around are endless plains of rock, gravel, and sand, where temperatures are scorching by day and freezing by night. In the midst of this lies an oasis, a cool spring rimmed by shady date palms and gardens.

Some oasis people grow crops such as wheat, barley, apricots, and pistachio nuts. Others raise sheep or goats for their milk, meat, and fleece. Everyone eagerly awaits the date harvest, for dates provide both food and trade goods.

Life is most exciting when wandering nomads drop in to water their flocks, or when a camel caravan passes through to trade carpets and cloth for the produce of the oasis. Then is the time to strike bargains and exchange the latest news. Campfires burn late as people swap boasts, tell each other tales, and sing songs under the starry desert sky.

What would you celebrate if you lived in these places?
Choose one place and jot down some ideas for a festival there.
Make a poster or brochure to advertise your festival.

The children will: □ interpret to note detail   □ jot to record ideas   □ expand to create a poster or brochure

Read the story. At the end of each part, write answers to the questions before you continue to read.

Ginny was the first to feel the rain. Just a couple of drops, plip-plop on the top of her head. If she'd been as busy looking around as the other kids were, she might not have noticed it either.

"Hey," she said to the boy ahead, "it's raining!" No answer. Maybe Joseph didn't know she was talking to him. She tugged on his arm, but he pulled away and started walking even faster through the woods.

By the time the others did notice the rain, it was really pouring.

"Let's turn back," grumbled Fiona. "I'm soaked."

"We can't turn back," said Joseph. "We went all the way back to camp to get lettuce to feed those baby rabbits we found. If they had a mother, they'd be down a rabbit hole, not in a cave. We can't let them starve."

So the group trudged on.

Ginny could smell the wet leaves and the tree bark around them. In the distance she heard the rumble of thunder.

"Is it ever getting dark," said Troy.

"Which way are we going?" said Fiona.

"This way," answered Joseph.

"But I thought the cave was over there," said Troy.

The kids fell silent. There was no getting around it. They were lost.

What do you think will happen next? Why do you think so?

But Ginny wasn't. "Follow me," she called out. "I know the way."

She set off, touching the tree trunks as she went, feeling for moss, as she had done on the way out from camp.

It felt good to be leading the group like this. She'd never been to a camp with sighted kids before, and the other campers treated her like a helpless baby. They wanted to help her all the time. "I can do it myself," Ginny would tell them when they opened the door

for her. "I can find it myself," she'd say when they tried to guide her to the right table at lunch. "Please let me alone!" she'd mutter when they offered to pack her knapsack for her. Soon the other kids didn't talk to her very much anymore.

When they had asked her along on their hike they'd sounded pretty half-hearted. But Ginny had gone anyway. It was better than staying behind. And now she was leading them back to the cave.

The children will: □ hypothesize to predict events

But when they got there, the baby rabbits were gone.

"What's happened to them?" cried Fiona.

Ginny crouched down. On the damp sandy floor she felt big tracks among little ones. "Looks like their mother came for them," she said, smiling.

"Maybe we should wait here until the storm's over," suggested Joseph.

"No way," said Troy. "The counsellors would take a fit."

The way back was darker and scarier. The wind whistled around them and blew branches into their path. Joseph tripped and fell. "Ouch! My knee!" he cried.

Ginny turned towards his voice. "Here, grab my arm," she said.

With Joseph holding onto Ginny's arm and leaning heavily against her, the group stumbled on. Every few steps Ginny stopped to touch tree trunks and cock her head, as if listening for something.

"Hurry up, Ginny," Fiona called. "Why do you keep stopping and touching everything?"

What do you think will happen next? Why do you think so?

A crack of lightning lit the forest. Thunder rumbled all around them. Ginny strained to listen.

"Did you hear that?" she asked Joseph. "Voices. It must be a search party looking for us."

Joseph just shook his head. All he heard was the thunder.

Ginny started walking faster, pulling Joseph along and shouting, "Here, we're over here! Just stay put and keep calling so I can find you!"

"That's funny," Troy said. "They're looking for *us* and yet you're saying you'll find *them*."

"It's not so funny," Fiona retorted. "In the dark Ginny's ears can see better than their eyes!"

Ginny smiled and set off, straight for the shouts of "Halloo! Halloo!" And then, suddenly, they were together, lost and found campers hugging and crying and laughing together.

"Ginny did it, Ginny led us back, Ginny knew the way," Fiona kept babbling, and then she stopped. "How did you know which way to go?" she asked.

"The moss," Ginny explained. "Moss grows on the north side of trees, so when I felt it on the far side of the trunks on the way out to the cave I knew we were heading north. On the way back I just did the opposite."

Share your predictions with a friend. Talk about why you made those predictions, and how the predictions helped you read the story.

The children will: ☐ hypothesize to predict events   ☐ talk to compare and justify predictions

Read each sentence and write what is being described and what it is being compared to.

1. The flames played their merry tune, crackling and popping in the fireplace.

   _____

2. The truck spluttered and grumbled, reluctant to start.

   _____

3. The moon walks the night in her silvery gown.

   _____

4. Giant waves attacked the shore, and then retreated.

   _____

5. The grandfather clock stood watch in the hall, ready to strike warning.

   _____

Write your own comparisons for these things, making them come alive as a person.

_____

_____

_____

_____

_____

_____

Think of other things that you might compare to people. Write sentences or verses to describe them. Share your ideas with a friend.

The children will: ☐ interpret to note comparisons   ☐ extend to create comparisons

Read the descriptions and underline the comparisons that create pictures in your mind.

Malicious weather hid behind the curtain of cloud waiting for the perfect moment to spoil the picnic with a barrage of lightning spears.

The sun is a smoldering fire,
that creeps through the high gray plain,
And leaves not a bush of cloud
To blossom with flowers of rain.

From *Collected Poems* of Vachel Lindsay (Copyright 1914 by Macmillan Publishing Company, renewed 1942 by Elizabeth C. Lindsay)

Gilded by sun and striped by shade, the hillside looked like the back of some great slumbering beast. The long grass, as tawny and dense as fur, rippled as the wind stroked it with her gentle fingers.

Waves are wild horses
Watch them go
Galloping, galloping
Arching their broad gray backs
Tossing their foamy manes
As white as snow

Not far from shore, a huge bullfrog was sunning himself. He looked for all the world like a sleepy old grandfather dozing on a front porch. His lily pad, as comfortable as any rocking chair, bobbed gently as the breeze ruffled the glassy surface of the pond.

Write each comparison where you think it belongs in a chart, using these headings.

like	as . . . as	is, are	like people

Add to your chart other comparisons that you might use to create similar mind pictures. Share your chart with a friend.

The children will: □ interpret to identify word pictures □ jot to classify word pictures

Discuss with a friend the ideas and pictures that come to your mind as you read each of these lines.

In winter it rains cats and dogs.

Elephant clouds dance slowly around.

Good-bye sailing.

Jet trails with swirling tails.

We crunch over the powdery snow.

The winds whistle like calliopes.

Fireworks burn the August sky.

Choose one line and write it in the circle. Make a web by jotting all the ideas and pictures it makes you think of.

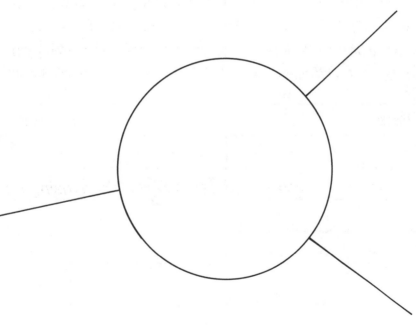

Make similar webs for other lines that you like.

The children will: □ talk to visualize ideas in pictures   □ choose and web to associate ideas

Read the article with a partner.

What is happening to football? The fun and excitement of the game are gone, and it's all because of artificial turf.

I recognize the benefits of the new playing surface. It is always flat and smooth, and is not damaged by weather or by the players' cleats. And it is certainly easier to take care of, since it doesn't have to be mowed or marked for every game.

But artificial turf has serious drawbacks. Many football injuries are caused by players falling on the harder playing surface. At least grass offers players a cushion when they fall. And sliding through water that sits invisible on top of the turf is far more dangerous than sliding through mud on a rain-soaked field.

Playing football on natural grass is part of the tradition of the game, and tradition is important. Some people argue that artificial turf improves the game because the ball bounces faster and farther, but that's not what football's really about. It's about the thrill of seeing a mud-covered ball fumbled and recovered three times in a row. Or a series of dazzling passing plays because running with the ball on a soggy field is nearly impossible. Artificial turf doesn't improve the game—it just improves the playing conditions.

I know that artificial turf is here to stay, and there's nothing I can do about it. But I sure miss the memorable plays that are gone with the grass—and the mud.

Complete the chart by listing facts and opinions from the article. Add your own facts and opinions about artificial turf.

Facts	Opinions

Discuss with your partner how you can prove if a statement is a fact or a opinion.

The children will: ☐ interpret to identify fact and opinion   ☐ list to summarize fact and opinion

Read the paragraph and think of words that could go in the blanks.

After that, they turned the yard behind the <u> 1 </u> into a rink. In the early winter, after the <u> 2 </u> froze, they cut the grass short. Then, using a <u> 3 </u> sprinkler, they flooded the ground with layer after layer of ice. Wayne's father added <u> 4 </u> and a huge spotlight. He put up <u> 5 </u> as obstacles for Wayne to skate patterns around. And over the years he put Wayne through all kinds of drills and <u> 6 </u> exercises. Many of these <u> 7 </u> ideas became <u> 8 </u> in Canada only after the 1972 series between Canada and the Soviet Union.

List possible words that make sense for each blank on the lines.

1	2	3	4

5	6	7	8

Share your words with a partner. Then read the paragraph on page 243 of "Gretzky! Gretzky! Gretzky!" to find the exact words the author used. Write the exact words in the boxes and compare your choices with those of the author.

Excerpt from *Gretzky! Gretzky! Gretzky!* by Meguido Zola. Reprinted by permission of Grolier Limited.

The children will: ☐ hypothesize to predict and confirm word choice

Girls Can Play Too

I am ten years old and I play hockey in Peewee B. The problem is that I am a girl. Some of the boys thought that I just couldn't skate or do anything because I was a girl. But after they played with me for a few weeks they changed their minds. I am number 8. When I am on defense I like to be like Risto Siltanen or Denis Potvin. When I am on right wing I like to be like Mike Bossy or Willi Plett, and when I'm on left wing, I like to be like Guy LaFleur (known as "The Flower") or Jim Peplinski.

My hope for the future is becoming a coach, an assistant coach, or a general manager of one of the teams in the Alberta Junior Hockey League. Maybe in my spare time I'll play hockey. Someday I even hope the National Hockey League will let women play too.

Bindya Jilka
Grade 5
Lynnwood School

From *Magpie: A Magazine of Children's Literature*, Edmonton Public Schools, Edmonton, Alberta.

Jot down your reasons for allowing or not allowing girls to play on hockey teams with boys.

_____

_____

_____

_____

_____

Use your jot notes to write a letter to the N.H.L. or to a hockey organization in your community.

The children will: ☐ jot to record opinions ☐ expand to write a letter

Before they went to see Glinda, however, they were taken to a room of the Castle, where Dorothy washed her face and combed her hair, and the Lion shook the dust out of his mane, and the Scarecrow patted himself into his best shape, and the Woodman polished his tin and oiled his joints.

When they were all quite presentable they followed the soldier girl into a big room where the Witch Glinda sat upon a throne of rubies.

She was both beautiful and young to their eyes. Her hair was a rich red in color and fell in flowing ringlets over her shoulders. Her dress was pure white; but her eyes were blue, and they looked kindly upon the little girl.

"What can I do for you, my child?" she asked.

Dorothy told the Witch all her story; how the cyclone had brought her to the Land of Oz, how she had found her companions, and of the wonderful adventures they had met with.

"My greatest wish now," she added, "is to get back to Kansas, for Aunt Em will surely think something dreadful has happened to me, and that will make her put on mourning; and unless the crops are better this year than they were last I am sure Uncle Henry cannot afford it."

Glinda leaned forward and kissed the sweet, upturned face of the loving little girl.

"Bless your dear heart," she said, "I am sure I can tell you of a way to get back to Kansas." Then she added: "But, if I do, you must give me the Golden Cap."

"Willingly!" exclaimed Dorothy. "Indeed, it is of no use to me now, and when you have it you can command the Winged Monkeys three times."

"And I think I shall need their service just those three times," answered Glinda, smiling.

Dorothy then gave her the Golden Cap, and the Witch said to the Scarecrow, "What will you do when Dorothy has left us?"

"I will return to the Emerald City," he replied, "for Oz has made me its ruler and the people like me. The only thing that worries me is how to cross the hill of the Hammer-Heads."

"By means of the Golden Cap I shall command the Winged Monkeys to carry you to the gates of the Emerald City," said Glinda, "for it would be a shame to deprive the people of so wonderful a ruler."

Turning to the Tin Woodman, she asked, "What will become of you when Dorothy leaves this country?"

He leaned on his axe and thought a moment. Then he said, "The Winkies were very kind to me, and wanted me to rule over them after the Wicked Witch died. I am fond of the Winkies, and if I could get back again to the country of the West I should like nothing better than to rule over them forever."

"My second command to the Winged Monkeys," said Glinda, "will be that they carry you safely to the land of the Winkies. Your brains may not be so large to look at as those of the Scarecrow, but you are really brighter than he is—when you are well-polished—and I am sure you will rule the Winkies wisely and well."

Then the Witch looked at the big, shaggy Lion and asked, "When Dorothy has returned to her own home, what will become of you?"

"Over the hill of the Hammer-Heads," he answered, "lies a grand old forest, and all the beasts that live there have made me their King. If I could only get back to this forest I would pass my life very happily there."

"My third command to the Winged Monkeys," said Glinda, "shall be to carry you to your forest. Then, having used up the powers of the Golden Cap, I shall give it to the King of the Monkeys, that he and his band may thereafter be free forevermore."

The Scarecrow and the Tin Woodman and the Lion now thanked the Good Witch earnestly for her kindness, and Dorothy exclaimed, "You are certainly as good as you are beautiful! But you have not yet told me how to get back to Kansas."

"Your Silver Shoes will carry you over the desert," replied Glinda. "If you had known their power you could have gone back to your Aunt Em the very first day you came to this country."

"But then I should not have had my wonderful brains!" cried the Scarecrow. "I might have passed my whole life in the farmer's cornfield."

"And I should not have had my lovely heart," said the Tin Woodman. "I might have stood rusted in the forest till the end of the world."

"And I should have lived a coward forever," declared the Lion, "and no beast in all the forest would have had a good word to say to me."

"This is all true," ___1___ Dorothy, "and I am ___2___ I was of use ___3___ these good friends. But ___4___ that each of them ___5___ had what he most ___6___ , and each is happy ___7___ having a kingdom to ___8___ besides, I think I ___9___ like to go back ___10___ Kansas."

"The Silver Shoes," ___11___ the Good Witch, "have ___12___ powers. And one of ___13___ most curious things about ___14___ is that they can ___15___ you to anyplace in ___16___ world in three steps, ___17___ each step will be ___18___ in the wink of ___19___ eye. All you have ___20___ do is to knock ___21___ heels together three times ___22___ command the shoes to ___23___ you wherever you wish ___24___ go."

"If that is ___25___ ," said the child joyfully, " ___26___ will ask them to ___27___ me back to Kansas ___28___ once."

She threw her ___29___ around the Lion's neck ___30___ kissed him, patting his ___31___ head tenderly. Then she ___32___ the Tin Woodman, who ___33___ weeping in a way ___34___ dangerous to his joints. ___35___ she hugged the soft, ___36___ body of the Scarecrow ___37___ her arms instead of ___38___ his painted face, and ___39___ she was crying herself ___40___ this sorrowful parting from her loving comrades.

Glinda the Good stepped down from her ruby throne to give the little girl a good-bye kiss, and Dorothy thanked her for all the kindness she had shown to her friends and herself.

Dorothy now took Toto up solemnly in her arms, and having said one last good-bye she clapped the heels of her shoes together three times, saying, "Take me home to Aunt Em!"

Paint It!
Weave It!
Carve It!

1. The Group of Seven were artists who became famous because of the new and exciting way they painted the landscapes of Canada. Find pictures of their work in art books and choose one that you like. Write a description of the scene in the painting, or use it as a setting to tell or write a story. Share your story and the picture with some friends.

2. Have you ever "felt blue" or "seen red"? Write a poem or story about a time when you felt happy, sad, frustrated, . . . using color to describe your mood and feelings. Paint a picture for your poem or story, using the same colors.

3. Some totem poles of Northwest Coast Indians tell family stories or legends through carved pictures. Find out about totem poles. What rules are there about designing totem poles? How are plants and animals used as symbols?
Draw or make a totem pole for your family. Display it with a chart or caption explaining what each part of the totem pole means.

4. With some friends, create an Artists' Studio. Bring in egg cartons, boxes, straws, rocks, wool, colored paper, and other items you can use to create your own two-dimensional or three-dimensional works of art.

The children will: ☐ choose to complete unit activities

5. Find out about different kinds of weavings by interviewing someone who weaves or by finding information in books. Practise some different weavings, using yarn or string, and show your friends how to do them.

6. With a partner, read *Paddle to the Sea* by H.C. Holling. Create a diorama to show one of Paddle to the Sea's adventures. Write a short caption telling what is happening and display it with your diorama.

7. Work with a group of friends and choose a story you would like to perform as a puppet play. Make your own puppets (from socks, paper bags, wooden spoons, . . .) and a puppet stage (from a large cardboard box or a table). Present the play to your classmates.

8. Choose some music that you like and listen to it. Draw or paint a picture that shows what is happening in the music, or how it makes you feel. Share your music and picture with a friend. Does your friend see or feel the same thing?

9. Many animals such as zebras and raccoons have interesting designs on their bodies. Research to find others that have unusual designs.
Create a display of drawings or paintings that show only the designs, not the animals. Hold a contest for your classmates to see who can correctly identify the most animals from the designs.

10. Find a book in the library about painting, carving, or weaving. Here are some you might enjoy reading.

A Prairie Boy's Winter, by William Kurelek.
Binky and the Bamboo Brush, by Adelle LaRouche.
The Weaver's Gift, by Kathryn Lasky.
There's a Rainbow in My Closet, by Patti Stren.
What To Do Till the Garbageman Arrives, by Ruth Johnson.

The children will: ☐ choose to complete unit activities

Read the article, then complete the chart and answer the questions.

With just a dab of red, yellow, and blue paint, artists can create many of the colors they will use in their paintings.

Red, yellow, and blue are called **primary colors**. Mixed together they make **secondary colors**. Combining red with yellow makes orange. Mixing yellow with blue makes green, and mixing blue with red makes violet. Even more colors can be made by combining primary and secondary colors together. For example, orange mixed with blue makes brown.

The colors black and white are also important. If you look closely at a painting, you will usually see different shades and tints of each color used. A **shade** of a color is created by adding black to that color. Black mixed with red creates dark reds, like crimson and maroon. A **tint** of a color is created by adding white to that color. White mixed with red creates light reds, like pink and rose.

Artists learn which combinations of colors to use in painting a bouquet of roses or a stormy sky by experience and by experimenting. An artist's palette is a rainbow of possibilities. The next time you paint a picture, try combining different colors to get the ones you want.

COLORS	Red	Yellow	Blue	White	Black
Red	▨				
Yellow		▨			
Blue			▨		
White				▨	
Black					▨

What colors would you mix to get different shades of green?

_____

What colors would you mix to get different tints of brown?

_____

Work with a partner to list all the names you know for different shades and tints of red, blue, yellow, green, orange, brown, . . . Share your list with your classmates.

The children will:　☐ interpret to complete a chart　☐ list to generate color words

Complete the diagram by writing words that describe each character.

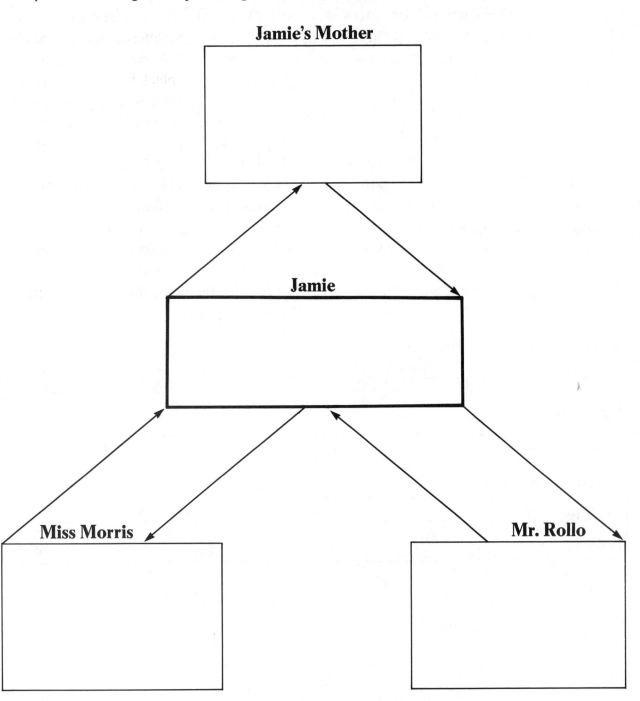

Jamie's Mother

Jamie

Miss Morris

Mr. Rollo

On the arrows, write words that tell how the character felt about Jamie and how he felt about them.

Share your diagram with a friend.

The children will: ☐ list to identify characteristics ☐ diagram to web relationships among characters

Marc trudged through the falling snow to the old wooden <u>synagogue</u>, where all the boys of the town gathered to study. As he walked, he thought about what his mother had told him. It was his duty to study the <u>Torah</u> so he would know the history and customs of the Jewish people.

Marc's heart thumped louder and faster as he approached the door. His teacher, the <u>rabbi</u>, was a serious scholar and made no allowances for <u>frivolity</u> or inattention. What was he going to do when he found that Marc had drawn pictures all over the paper, instead of using it for his homework?

He opened the door and went in. The other students tittered as he walked by, but they kept their faces hidden behind their books. No one wanted to risk a <u>reprimand</u> from the rabbi.

Write what you think the words mean and the clues that gave you the meaning.

1. synagogue—meaning: _____

   clues: _____

2. Torah—meaning: _____

   clues: _____

3. rabbi—meaning: _____

   clues: _____

4. frivolity—meaning: _____

   clues: _____

5. reprimand—meaning: _____

   clues: _____

Share your ideas with a friend and together check your meanings in a dictionary.

The children will: ☐ interpret to identify meaning from context ☐ write to show meaning in a different context ☐ read to verify meanings in the dictionary

Skim the article to find the headings. Jot down the information you think you will find under each heading. Read the article to check your predictions.

ALEX BEGINS TO DRAW

Alex Colville began to draw when he was nine years old. He was sick with pneumonia for several months, and drawing helped him to pass the time. Like most kids, Alex liked to draw cars, boats, and airplanes. But he drew with a difference. He planned his drawings in the same way an engineer draws plans for a bridge—with sketches and blueprints.

ALEX LEARNS ABOUT ART

When he was in high school, Alex took drawing lessons for the first time and began to draw people as well as objects. Stanley Royle, an art teacher from Mount Allison University, visited one of his classes and encouraged him to study art. Later, when Alex went to university he studied with Royle, and decided to become a professional artist.

Alex's dream was interrupted by World War II. He joined the army and became a war artist. In his sketches and watercolors he recorded the everyday life of the soldiers and the destruction of battle.

After the war, Alex visited art galleries in Europe to look at original masterpieces of famous painters, which he had only seen in art books.

When he returned to Canada, Alex became an art teacher. However, he soon gave up teaching so that he could devote all his time to his painting.

Photograph by Arnaud Maggs

ALEX BECOMES A PROFESSIONAL

Alex Colville's favorite subjects for his work are his family and the landscape near his home in Nova Scotia. He gets ideas for his paintings from real-life situations of ordinary people—a family trip to the beach, a young girl skipping in a schoolyard, a boy greeting his dog after school.

Colville still draws sketches and diagrams to plan a painting, the way he did when he was a boy. Then using oils, acrylics, or tempera (paint mixed with egg yolk), he paints the picture, realistically, with small, precise brush strokes.

Today, Colville's paintings hang in famous art galleries, and people come to admire his masterpieces. Perhaps some young person studying his work will learn from him, the way he learned from the European artists.

How do headings help readers? How do they help authors?

The children will: ☐ skim to note subheads ☐ jot to record predictions ☐ read to verify predictions

Look at the different styles of art. How are the owl details the same?
How are they different?

1

©Glen Loates 1987.

2

Kenojuak, *The Enchanted Owl*, 1960
Reproduced with permission of the West Baffin Eskimo Cooperative Limited,
Cape Dorset, NWT.

3

Trademark of the Young Naturalist Foundation, reproduced with permission.

4

Choose another animal and find pictures of it in different styles of art.

The children will: ☐ observe to appreciate artists' styles ☐ observe to note similarities and differences in artists' styles

Reread "Pitseolak: Pictures out of My Life."
Jot the important information for
each heading.

My Family

_____
_____
_____
_____
_____
_____

Homes

_____
_____
_____
_____
_____
_____

Fun and Games

_____
_____
_____
_____
_____
_____

My Art

_____
_____
_____
_____
_____
_____

Share your jot notes with a friend and compare your information.

The children will: ☐ reread and jot to classify and summarize information   ☐ talk to compare information

Poems from Pictures

Write a poem for each picture.

Artist Unknown, Moose Factory

_____
_____
_____
_____
_____
_____
_____
_____
_____
_____

_____
_____
_____
_____
_____
_____
_____
_____
_____

Edward Hardisty, Moose Factory

Read your poems to some friends.

The children will: ☐ imitate to create a poem

People everywhere enjoy listening to a good story. Here are some suggestions to help you become a good storyteller.

First of all, you need a good story to tell—an adventure story with action and excitement, or a mystery with lots of suspense, or a humorous story with funny characters and events.

Once you have chosen a story, read it over several times so that you really know it and can tell it in your own words. Then think about your story carefully.

—What are the characters like? How are they feeling? What would they sound like?
—What is the mood? Is it funny? Scary? Exciting? Sad?
—Where does the story take place? What does the setting look like? What kind of day is it?

As you think about your story in this way, you'll get ideas for tones of voice and facial expressions that will create different characters and moods for your listeners.

Keep your audience in mind as you think about your story. To make the characters and events come alive, think about how you can use your body as well as your voice so that your listeners can *see,* as well as *hear,* what's happening.

—What can you do with your hands and feet to show that a character is impatient? angry? riding a horse? climbing a ladder?
—How can you move your arms and shoulders to show that a character is swimming? waking up? rocking a baby?

You've thought about the story and the audience, now think about yourself. How do you want to tell your story? Do you want to use props and puppets? Do you want to add sound effects and background music? Or would you rather not use any of these things? You don't have to. The important thing is to choose a way that suits you, so that you enjoy telling your story and your audience enjoys listening to it. That's what makes a good storyteller.

Use these ideas to tell a story to some friends.

The children will: ☐ interpret to obtain information ☐ talk to narrate a story

Complete the web with words that describe one picture.

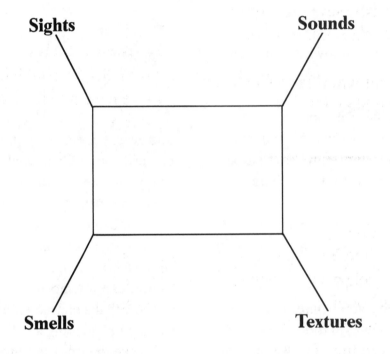

Use the ideas in your web to help you write about the setting, characters, and scene in your story.

Share your story with your classmates.

The children will: ☐ web to record descriptive details   ☐ expand to write a story

The Footprint

There it was! Right there in the sand. Right where the ocean stopped making waves.

It was big! As big as a small giant's. I bet giants go to the beach too.

Or maybe it was Big Foot, just down here for a hot dog roast.

Robinson Crusoe saw a footprint too! I read that in a book from the library.

(Mom said that when I grow up my feet will be even bigger!)

Tree Wish

It won't be long now.

Even though there's still snow on my branches I can feel spring coming— way down at my roots.

I hope those two birds come back and build a nest in me. They certainly brighten up my days.

And they're such good company.

Dream Car

In the back of the magazine it says, "You too, can build the car of your dreams."

If I start with that old truck out back . . .

The Horse's Friend

I have a little friend with black hair and we have a secret. We are the only two who can see how really beautiful and spacious our meadow is.

Looking Cat

"There is nothing nicer than sitting in a window and watching the world go by.

I have seven windows.

I see something different from each one."

Create your own "criss-cross applesauce," using one of these captions, a photograph, and a drawing or painting.

Black Ice Publishers for selections from *Criss-Cross Applesauce* by Tony King and Children, text by Tomie de Paola. Copyright ᶜ 1978. Reprinted by permission of Tony King.

The children will: ☐ interpret to choose a commentary ☐ illustrate to create a pictorial commentary

Complete this form to show another way that the book report could be written.

Title: _____

Author: _____

Illustrator: _____

What the book is about: _____

_____

_____

_____

_____

_____

_____

My response to the book: _____

_____

_____

_____

_____

_____

_____

_____

Share your report with a classmate.
Which kind of book report do you like better? Why?

The children will: ☐ write to complete a book report form ☐ assess to compare different kinds of book reports

Read the reviews and discuss them with a partner.

Different Dragons by Jean Little.
Penguin, 1986.
$12.95 cloth 0-670-80836-9

Jean Little continues to demonstrate her acute understanding of the emotional lives of children. In *Different Dragons* her main character, Ben Tucker, is a shy youngster who would prefer to remain in familiar territory rather than adventure forth towards new frontiers. But Ben must spend a weekend with his Aunt Rose, whom he knows only slightly, in the house where she and Ben's father grew up. Despite the boy's efforts to create a protective wall around himself again, this time he is intruded upon. First comes the terrifying (for Ben) golden retriever Gulliver Gallant. Next is the brash daughter of the next-door neighbor who has no time for Ben's fear of dogs. Somehow, all on his own, Ben must handle and overcome these disruptions in his life.

In narrating Ben's small victory, Jean Little describes experiences common to many children. She does it succinctly and eloquently. Jean Little is one of our great children's writers. Recommended for Grades 4 to 6

From *Children's Books News 1986* by permission of the Canadian Children's Book Centre.

When the Wolves Sang. OWL, 1981.

What's it like to camp in the wild among wolves who've never seen a human before? Discover exactly how wild wolves behave in this true story illustrated with color photographs. (Ages 6–10), 36 pages, 14 x 17½ cm, hard cover, $5.95.

From *OWL Magazine*, September 1981, by permission of the Young Naturalist Foundation.

Cleaver, Elizabeth
The Enchanted Caribou.
Il. by author. ISBN 0-689-31170-2.
New York: Atheneum, 1985. 30 pp. $9.95.

A young Inuit woman, lost in fog, is rescued and sheltered by a hunter. Later, tricked by a Shaman, she is turned into a white caribou. Through skill and magic, the hunter finds her and breaks the enchantment. This legend is illustrated in a stunning approximation of shadow-puppetry beautifully suited to its stark setting and dream-like quality. Directions for creating the story as a shadow puppet play are included. Ages 8–11.

From *Childhood Education*, May/June 1986, by permission of the Association for Childhood Education International.

Suzuki, David
Looking At Insects
Toronto: Stoddart, 1985.
$8.95 Paper 0-7737-5062-2
Illustrations by R. Tukerman.
Reading Level Gr. 4
Interest Level Gr. 4–8

This informative, clearly written book provides a very close look at the world of insects. There is a lot of information and enjoyment in this excellent science discovery book. For instance, do you know how the Dauber wasp feeds its young? It's incredible!

From *Our Choice Catalogue 1986/87* by permission of the Canadian Children's Book Centre.

Think about these questions as you discuss the reviews.

Who was the review written for?
What type of information was given in all the reviews? Why is this information important?
Which book would you like to read? Why?
If you have read one of these books, do you agree with the review? Why or why not?

The children will: ☐ interpret and talk to assess book reviews ☐ talk to explain and justify conclusions

A Poem Inside a Paragraph

What poem can you set free from this paragraph?

Last night he had sat in his room for hours watching the snowflakes whirl around the gas lamps in the street, causing strange halos to form around the glowing lights. He had looked at the people hurrying to their houses, dark against the snow and hunched from the cold. He loved to see their strange shapes and especially those of the carts drawn by the horses or mules. As he watched, he drew pictures, using paper from his schoolbook and some old paper bags his mother had given him.

Excerpt from *The Boy Who Drew People Upside Down* by Jean Friedman.
Reprinted by permission of the author.

Underline the words in the passage that help make pictures in your mind.
Choose some of the words and arrange them in a found poem.
Write a title for your poem.

_____

Share your poem with some friends.

The children will: □ interpret to identify word pictures　□ choose and arrange to create a found poem

Skim the article and complete the chart.

Name and Location	Materials Used	Important Details about the Sculpture	What the Sculptor Wanted to Show

Use this kind of chart to summarize information about other sculptures you have seen or read about.

The children will: ☐ skim to locate information ☐ jot to complete a chart

Carving Stone

Jot down what the artist is doing in each picture.

1.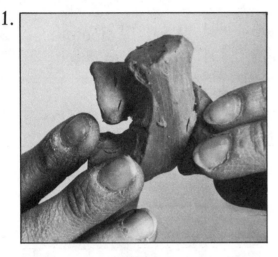

   _____

   _____

   _____

   _____

   _____

   _____

   _____

2.

   _____

   _____

   _____

   _____

   _____

3.

   _____

   _____

   _____

   _____

   _____

The children will: ☐ observe and jot to note details

4.

5.

6.

Photographs by David Anderson

Use your jot notes to write a summary about how a stone sculpture is made.
Share your summary with a friend.

What do you think of when you hear the word "picture"? Chances are you think of a painting, a drawing, or a photograph. But there is another kind of picture that is woven out of colored threads. It is called a *tapestry*.

A tapestry can be a picture of almost anything. There are tapestries that show people, animals, flowers, hunting scenes, battle scenes, and scenes from history and legend. Some tapestries are single pictures, and others are sets of pictures that tell a story, like the Unicorn Tapestries. A tapestry can be any size—from as small as a cushion to as big as a wall—and it can be made of wool, silk, cotton, or linen threads.

It takes an artist and a weaver to make a tapestry. The artist's task is to draw a picture the same size as the finished tapestry will be, with all the details and colors exactly as they will be on the tapestry. This picture is called a *cartoon*. It is the design or pattern that the weaver follows to make the tapestry.

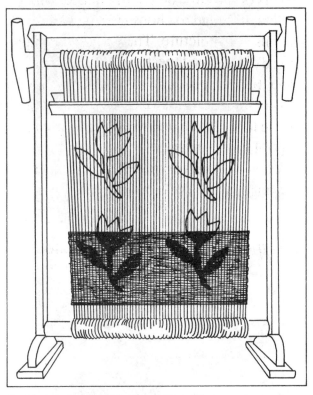

Cartoon design traced on warp threads

Cartoon

To see what happens next, you must go into the weaver's workshop. First, the weaver sets up the loom to weave a tapestry the size of the cartoon. Long woollen threads are

fastened so they run the length of the loom. These are called the *warp* threads, and they form the base of the tapestry. Next, the weaver draws the outline of the whole cartoon in dark ink directly on the warp threads. This shows exactly the shape of every detail of the cartoon that the weaver must follow. Now the weaving can begin.

The weaver sits at the loom, weaving colored threads over and under the warp threads to create the picture. These colored threads are called the *weft* threads. The

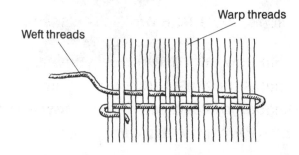

Warp threads

Weft threads

The children will: ☐ interpret to obtain information

The children will: ☐ interpret to obtain information ☐ summarize to explain how to make a tapestry ☐ summarize to explain opinions ☐ talk to formulate and explain opinions

colors of the cartoon tell the weaver which colors of thread to choose for the various details of the picture. The weaver completes one detail of the tapestry, like a tree or a deer, before beginning another. If the tapestry is very large, several weavers sit side by side at the loom. Each one works on only one part of the tapestry.

The weaving is done from the back or "wrong" side of the tapestry, so the weaver looks in a mirror set in front of the loom to check the front side of the tapestry. Many tapestries are so neatly woven that the back looks almost as good as the front.

It takes a lot of time to do work as fine as this. In olden days when people ordered large sets of tapestries they sometimes had to wait ten years for them to be finished. And many weavers ruined their eyesight creating those beautiful woven pictures.

List the materials that can be used in tapestry-making.

_____

_____

_____

Summarize the steps in making a tapestry.

_____

_____

_____

_____

_____

_____

_____

_____

Discuss the article with your classmates.

What new information did you learn about tapestries?
What is the most interesting or unusual information you learned?
What else would you like to know about tapestries?

Which Words?

Read this part of the story and think of words that would fit in the blanks.

To make the first, high thread ___1___ hold the web, she had to ___2___ up high and then throw herself ___3___ across the dark air, hoping she ___4___ land safe on the other side. ___5___ work was like riding the flying ___6___ in the circus. It was like ___7___ bridges, too, because each part of ___8___ web helped hold up every other ___9___ in the air. And it was ___10___ singing, because she spun her thread ___11___ of her body, as the singer ___12___ her voice out of her throat. ___13___ the singer's voice runs up and ___14___ the music, la-la-la!, so the patterns ___15___ Leese's thread ran up and down ___16___ round in lovely curves and angles. ___17___ had learned how to weave her ___18___ , now. Some of her webs had ___19___ like leaves and flowers, imitated from ___20___ carpet; some had designs like huntsmen, hounds, and horns, copied from the painting on the wall.

Write a word that would fit and make sense for each blank.

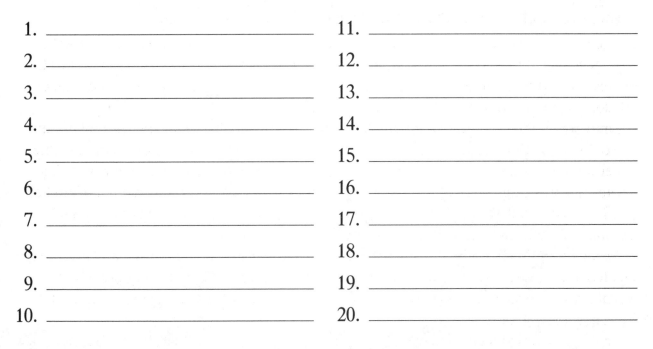

1. _____
2. _____
3. _____
4. _____
5. _____
6. _____
7. _____
8. _____
9. _____
10. _____

11. _____
12. _____
13. _____
14. _____
15. _____
16. _____
17. _____
18. _____
19. _____
20. _____

Share your words with a partner. Then read the paragraph on page 296 of "Leese Webster" to compare the author's words with yours.

Excerpt from *Leese Webster* by Ursula Le Guin. Copyright © 1979 by Ursula Le Guin. Reprinted by permission of Atheneum Publishers, a division of Macmillan, Inc.

The children will: ☐ hypothesize to predict and confirm word choice

When Emily Carr was a child, she gave herself the nickname "Small" since she was the youngest in the family. She called her two older sisters "Middle" and "Bigger."

Emily received fond attention from her sisters as the baby of the family, but she felt different from them. While they did well at school, Emily found it a struggle to sit still at her desk. She longed to be outside playing in the country fields and woods. While her sisters liked to dress up and play Ladies in the garden, Emily quickly grew tired of this game and wandered off alone to climb a tree or wade in the brook's cold water.

Emily sometimes felt cross with her sisters because they would not join in her kind of fun. She often found that the animals around her home made more interesting companions. One of her favorite pastimes was to sit on the woodpile in the cow yard and sing. She would sing whatever words came into her mind as she went along. Soon the rooster would jump into her lap. The cow would wander over and stand close by, chewing her cud. The hens and ducks and rabbits would cock their heads as if to catch the sweet music.

Sweet music? Well, Emily thought so, but no one else seemed to appreciate it. "Small! Stop that hideous noise for goodness sakes!" Bigger came rushing into the yard in a great huff. "Small, you simply cannot make such a row! The neighbors will think someone is in trouble. Now, come along for breakfast."

Emily was a little bit embarrassed, but mostly she was obstinate. "The animals like my singing," she replied, and launched into another song. This time she sang a little LOUDER than usual, and the cow chewed her cud faster. Emily thought that this was a sure sign that the cow approved of her singing. "See?" she glared at her sister. Eventually, Emily did go in for her breakfast, and she was scolded about her loud singing there too.

Singing to the cow was fun, but deep down in her heart Emily wanted to have a dog. A dog would be so much more of a companion, but it was not allowed. Emily decided to draw a picture of the sort of dog that she would like to have. She carefully tore open a brown paper bag along the creases and flattened it out. Then, with a charred stick from the fireplace, she drew a puppy with large friendly eyes and a happy tail. As she drew, Emily thought, "This is fun! I would like to draw lots of things."

Emily's family was so ___1___ by her sketch that ___2___ was allowed to take ___3___ classes. Emily made herself ___4___ easel by snugly tying ___5___ branches from the cherry ___6___ that stood by her ___7___ window. She put a ___8___ of her father, which ___9___ had drawn, on her ___10___ and stepped back to ___11___ it. "Now I feel ___12___ a real artist," she ___13___ happily to herself.

Now ___14___ Emily had discovered how ___15___ fun it was to ___16___ pictures, she could not ___17___. She even found herself ___18___ at school when she ___19___ have been doing her ___20___.

BANG! A ruler slapped ___21___ on Emily's desk. Emily ___22___ out of her daydreaming ___23___ see her teacher glowering ___24___ at her. "Emily! If ___25___ catch you drawing faces ___26___ your apron one more ___27___, I shall send you ___28___. Now pay attention."

Poor Emily, ___29___ was forever getting into ___30___ with her parents and ___31___ and teachers. They all ___32___ her dearly, but they ___33___ her to behave like ___34___ proper young lady. Emily ___35___ simply not interested in ___36___. She found it impossible ___37___ act with good manners. ___38___ found it impossible to ___39___ her dresses tidy and ___40___. It seemed so difficult to be good.

Sometimes to get away from all the scolding people, Emily would ride her old pony, Johnny, into the countryside. "Take me into the woods, Johnny. Take me away, far away." Emily let Johnny find his own way. He always found special places deep in the forest where Emily was awed by the beauty of nature. She would sit quiet and still to observe every detail. She wanted to absorb the feeling of the woods because they seemed so special to her. "Canada is beautiful," she whispered to Johnny. "Some day when I am really an artist I shall be able to paint these mysterious forests."

Excerpt from *Emily Carr* by Marion Endicott. Copyright © 1981 by Marion Endicott. Reprinted by permission of the Women's Educational Press, Toronto.

JOURNEYS

O Canada!

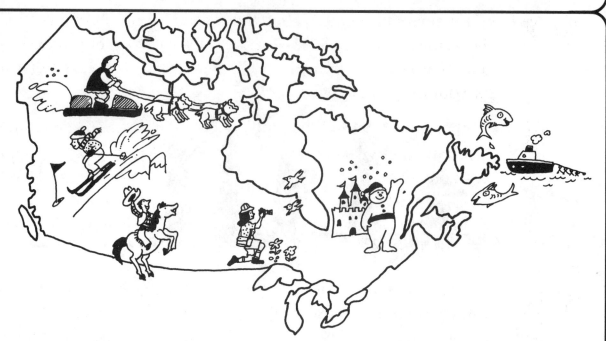

 1. The Trans-Canada Highway, at 7821 km, is the world's longest national road. Find out all you can about when, why, and how it was built. On a map, show the route the highway takes across Canada and the places it goes through. Use the map to help you tell some classmates about the highway.

 2. Find and listen to recordings of Canadian folk songs like "Something to Sing About" by Oscar Brand. Choose the one you like the best and sing it with some friends. Make up some new verses for the song.

3. Canada is famous for many sports, some of which began here. Find out about one of these sports and a Canadian who is famous because of it. Organize your information in a chart or web and share it with some friends. This list might help you—skiing, ice hockey, curling, lacrosse, basketball.

 4. The place where you live has an interesting past. Use your public library's newspaper files, local history books, or interview some older residents, to find out about some important event. Write your own newspaper report about the event and post it for others to read.

The children will: ☐ choose to complete unit activities

5. Each province and territory in Canada has a coat of arms which shows the history, beliefs, and hopes of each. Find out what the coat of arms for your province means. Then design a coat of arms for your own family or school.

6. Dances are an important part of the heritage of Canada's many different ethnic groups. With a partner or small group, find out how to do one of these special dances. Family members, friends, or books can help you. Practise the dance and present it to your classmates. Some you might wish to learn are the polka, schottische, calypso, hora, and the tarantella.

7. Are you a stamp collector? Much of Canada's story is shown on postage stamps. Choose some stamps which picture events in Canadian history. Research the events to learn more about them. Show the stamps to your classmates and tell about them.

8. Work with a partner to make a book of poems about Canada. Find or write poems which tell about Canada's scenery, weather, people, animals, and customs. Use your own drawings or pictures from magazines to illustrate the poems.

9. Canada has many heroes. Some are famous across the country, while others are known in their own area. Find out about the brave deeds of one of them. Then imagine you are that person and tape record your story. Tell who you are, what happened, and how you felt.

10. Find a book in the library about people and places of Canada. Here are some you might enjoy reading.

> *All Aboard! A Cross Canada Adventure,* by Barbara O'Kelly and Beverly Allison.
> *Cariboo Runaway,* by Frances Duncan.
> *Michi's New Year,* by Shelley Tanaka.
> *She Shoots She Scores!,* by Heather Kellerhals-Stewart.
> *The General,* by Frank Etherington.
> *The New Wind Has Wings: Poems from Canada,* compiled by Marie Alice Downie and Barbara Robertson.

The children will: ☐ choose to complete unit activities

Cross Canada Quiz

Answer the questions to find out what you know about Canada.

1. What are the names of three Canadian provinces?

   _____

2. Name the province that is an island.

   _____

3. What is the capital city of Canada?

   _____

4. What is the name of one provincial capital city besides your own?

   _____

5. Canada is bounded by three oceans. Name two of them.

   _____

6. What are the names of two of the Great Lakes?

   _____

7. What is the name of Canada's highest mountain range?

   _____

8. What crop are the prairie provinces known for?

   _____

9. Why do Canadians celebrate July 1?

   _____

10. Name the animal that is the symbol of Canada.

   _____

Discuss your answers with some friends. Find out the answers to questions you are not sure about.

The children will: □ jot to record answers to questions   □ talk to share and compare answers

Miller Services

Scan the photograph. Ask yourself three questions about it.
Then look at the photograph carefully and answer your questions.

What: _____   _____

_____   _____

_____   _____

Where: _____   _____

_____   _____

_____   _____

Why: _____   _____

_____   _____

_____   _____

Share your questions and answers with a partner.
Add to each other's answers if you can.

The children will: □ scan to "question" a photograph □ observe to note details and answer questions

Which of these resources might contain the information you want?

Table of Contents

Subject Card

917.8E   MOUNTAINS

Ellis, William S.

   The Majestic Rocky Mountains

     How the Rockies were formed, their location, and history.

    Also includes recreation and industry. Photographs.

   The National Geographic Society, 1976.   200 p.

The children will: ☐ skim to identify appropriate information

Encyclopedia Entry

ROCKY MOUNTAINS are the largest mountain system in North America. The Rocky Mountain Chain extends more than 4800 kilometres through Canada and the United States. In some places, it is 563 kilometres wide.

In Canada, the Rockies spread through Alberta, British Columbia, the Northwest Territories, and the Yukon Territory. The Canadian Rockies separate rivers flowing north to the Arctic Ocean from those that empty into the Pacific Ocean to the southwest. The Rocky Mountain Chain forms the Continental Divide, separating rivers that flow west to the Pacific Ocean from rivers that flow east to the Atlantic Ocean.

Tourists travel to the Rockies to enjoy the magnificent scenery. The region is famous for its snow-capped peaks, sparkling lakes, ski resorts, and wildlife. In Alberta, Banff and Jasper National Parks offer tourists some of the best scenic areas in Canada.

RANGES OF THE ROCKIES include the Canadian Rockies, which extent from the border north into British Columbia and Alberta, the Selwyn Mountains, the Mackenzie Range, the Southern Rockies, the Middle Rockies, and the Northern Rockies.

AGRICULTURE AND INDUSTRY. Cattle and sheep graze on mountain pastures during the summer and move to the warmer valleys in winter.

Lumbering and mining are important in the Northern and Canadian Rockies. Tourism is also an important industry for Rocky Mountain areas.

PLANT AND ANIMAL LIFE. Forests cover the lower slopes of the Rocky Mountains. Pines, firs, and spruces are most common at higher elevations.

Rocky Mountain Goats and Bighorn Sheep live above the timberline where trees cannot grow. Animals like bears and deer, live on the higher forested slopes. Chipmunks, coyote, and muskrats live in the grassy valleys. Many kinds of fish live in the mountain streams.

HISTORY. Most of the peaks of the Rockies were formed millions of years ago, during an upheaval of the earth's crust. The mountains contain fossils of animals that once lived in the sea, and rocks formed in the hot interior of the earth. The Rockies also include mountains that were once volcanic plateaus. Through the centuries, Rocky Mountain peaks have been cut into various formations by wind, rain, and glaciers.

Related Articles include:
Banff National Park
Bighorn Sheep
Jasper National Park
Rocky Mountain Goat

Find other resources in your library to help you answer your questions.

The children will: ☐ skim to identify appropriate information ☐ extend to locate other resources

Use the information in the photo essay to jot answers to the questions.
Share your ideas with a friend.

1. Why are machines like a combine harvester needed on prairie farms?

   _____

   _____

2. What are some activities for tourists in the Rockies? _____

   _____

   _____

3. How are the Arctic and the Canadian Shield the same? How are they
   different?

   _____

   _____

4. What occupations might people have on Canada's east coast?

   _____

   _____

5. What are the main industries in the six regions? _____

   _____

   _____

   _____

6. Which region would you most like to visit? Why? _____

   _____

   _____

7. What one sentence could you write to describe Canada?

   _____

   _____

The children will: ☐ jot to record answers to questions

Listen to information about the four places.
Write the main idea and two facts for each place.

Joggins, Nova Scotia

Main idea _____

Two facts _____

_____

Tadoussac, Quebec

Main idea _____

Two Facts _____

_____

Medicine Hat, Alberta

Main idea _____

Two facts _____

_____

Bella Coola, British Columbia

Main idea _____

Two facts _____

_____

Compare your answers with a friend.
Are some answers the same? Are some different? Why?

The children will: ☐ attend to identify main ideas and facts ☐ talk to share and compare answers

The names of Canadian towns, rivers, lakes, and mountains can tell us a lot about our history.

Many place names originated with Canada's Native people. The name Canada comes from *kanata,* a Huron-Iroquois word meaning village or settlement. Winnipeg comes from the Cree word *win-nipi,* which means murky water. Chilliwack, Ottawa, and Miramichi are examples of other places named from Indian languages.

Explorers and pioneers often named settlements after places in the countries they left behind. A map of the world will show many Canadian place names that originated in Europe, such as London, Banff, Laval, Hamburg, and Halicz.

People also named places for features of the land—the Grand Banks of Newfoundland and the Rocky Mountains—or what the land produced—Cherry Valley in Prince Edward Island and Uranium City in Saskatchewan.

Many places have been named for and by famous people, like Victoria, Vancouver, Hudson Bay, and Champlain. But there are also many places that were named after not-so-famous people. Peggy's Cove in Nova Scotia was named after the wife of a local settler, and Jasper, Alberta, was named for a clerk who ran a trading post there.

Places in Canada have also been named for events in our history. The Peace River in Alberta takes its name from nearby Peace Point, where the Cree and Beaver tribes settled a dispute about land. Bonanza Creek in the Yukon was the site of the gold discovery that started the Klondike Gold Rush.

There are thousands of place names in Canada. These names give us a record of our past and a rich heritage we can all share.

Complete the web to summarize the information from the article.

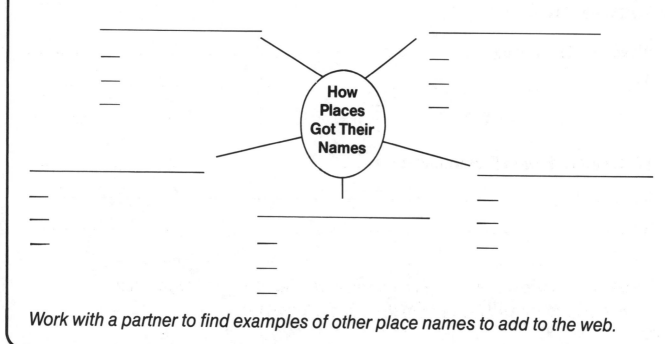

Work with a partner to find examples of other place names to add to the web.

The children will: □ web to summarize information □ jot to expand a web

Write what you liked about each poem and why you liked it.
Share your ideas with a partner.

Tofino, B.C. _____

_____

_____

The Yukon Swamplands _____

_____

_____

My Land _____

_____

_____

Sudbury Is _____

_____

_____

Nova Scotian Spring _____

_____

_____

It's Good to Live in Newfoundland _____

_____

_____

Work with your partner to write a poem about the place where you live.
Use the patterns and ideas from the poems to help you.

The children will: ☐ jot to explain and justify opinions ☐ imitate to create a poem

Making Moussaka

Ingredients

3 medium-sized eggplants
250mL butter
3 large onions, finely chopped
900g ground lamb or beef
45mL tomato paste
125mL beef bouillon
125mL chopped parsley
1mL basil
Salt and pepper to taste
90mL flour

1 L milk
4 eggs, beaten until frothy
Pinch of nutmeg
500mL ricotta cheese
250mL fine bread crumbs
250mL grated Parmesan cheese

Directions

1. Peel the eggplants and cut them into slices about 1cm thick. Heat 60mL of the butter in a skillet and brown the slices quickly over moderately high heat. Remove the eggplant slices and set aside.

2. Heat 60mL of butter in the same skillet and cook the onions until they are golden brown. Add the ground meat and cook ten minutes, stirring with a wooden spoon to break up the lumps of meat. In a small bowl, combine the tomato paste with the beef bouillon, parsley, basil, salt, and pepper. Stir this mixture into the meat and simmer over low heat, stirring frequently, until all the liquid has been absorbed. Set the mixture aside.

3. Preheat the oven to moderate (190°C).

4. Melt 125mL of butter in a heavy pot and blend in the flour, stirring with a wire whisk. Gradually pour the milk into the butter-flour mixture, stirring constantly. When the sauce is thickened and smooth, remove it from the heat. Cool slightly and stir in the beaten eggs, nutmeg, and ricotta cheese.

5. Grease a 30cm x 40cm pan and sprinkle the bottom lightly with bread crumbs. Arrange alternate layers of eggplant slices and meat mixture in the pan, sprinkling each layer with Parmesan cheese and bread crumbs. Pour the ricotta cheese sauce over the top and bake one hour, or until the top is golden. Remove from the oven and cool twenty to thirty minutes. Cut into squares and serve. Makes 8 to 10 servings.

Collect other ethnic recipes and make a heritage cookbook with your classmates.

The children will: ☐ interpret to compare spoken and written directions ☐ extend to create a heritage cookbook

Read the paragraph and think of words that could go in each blank.

But Chin Chiang ___1___ her by the hand, and they ___2___ down the stairs together—round and round, down, down, down, to the ___3___ street. The ___4___ of firecrackers exploded in their ears while the ___5___ crowd buzzed and hummed. Chin Chiang ___6___ his way forward, but Pu Yee pulled back. In the noise and confusion Chin Chiang let go of her hand, and ___7___ he came face to face with the dragon whose head was ___8___ in smoke.

List possible words that would make sense for each blank.

1	2	3	4

5	6	7	8

Share your words with a partner. Then read the paragraph on page 315 of "Chin Chiang and the Dragon's Dance" to find the exact words the author used. Write the exact words in the boxes.

Excerpt from *Chin Chiang and the Dragon's Dance* by Ian Wallace, Groundwood Books. 1984. Reprinted by permission of Douglas & McIntyre Ltd.

Reading/Writing/Speaking   Chin Chiang and the Dragon's Dance

The children will: ☐ hypothesize to predict and confirm word choice

Complete the chart by describing how Melanie felt during the different times in the story.

At the beginning	At the festival	At the end

Use the information from the chart to help you answer the questions.

How was Melanie different at the end of the story than she was at the beginning?

_____

_____

What happened at the festival to cause her to change?

_____

_____

How would Melanie have felt if she had decided to keep the stones?

_____

_____

What does Melanie's decision tell you about her?

_____

_____

Share your chart and answers with a friend.

The children will: ☐ jot to complete a chart   ☐ expand to write answers to questions

Read the news report and complete the chart.

Muir Swims Home

By D'Arcy McGovern
Toronto Star

The skies were gray and overcast over Toronto Harbour but the smile on Jocelyn Muir's face was as bright as a June sunrise.

Muir stepped ashore at the CNE's Aquarama site just after 11 a.m., August 29, 1987, becoming the first person ever to swim the entire distance around Lake Ontario, 521.5 nautical miles. She accomplished it in 60 days.

The swim raised more than $250,000 for research into multiple sclerosis, a disease that afflicts an estimated 50,000 Canadians.

The plucky 21-year-old University of Toronto student swam the last few metres amid the blare of boathorns and the cheers of hundreds of supporters who stood along the shore. When she emerged, tears mixed with the cold—6C (45F)—water of the lake and ran down a face tinted blue from the chill.

"This shouldn't have been possible," she said breathlessly, and hugged her coach. "It was really, really hard."

But Muir made it look easy, especially on the final day of her swim, knifing through the water with crisp, rapid strokes that averaged 76 a minute.

It's one more record to join the rest. Muir is also the youngest person ever to swim across Lake Ontario. She set that record when just 15. Last year she was the first person to swim the treacherous waters of Vancouver's Burrard Inlet.

Muir said it was the support of the sufferers from multiple sclerosis who followed her marathon that kept her going through the hard times.

"There were days when I'd come out of the water and they'd be sitting there and they'd start crying," she said. "I guess they said to themselves, 'Somebody out there who doesn't know me cares.'"

Among the onlookers cheerfully digging into slices of Muir's celebration cake were Don and Bernice Webb. Bernice, who has multiple sclerosis, had craned her neck from her wheelchair to catch a glimpse of Muir through the crowd.

"She's just fantastic," said Webb, showing off the cap that she'd asked Muir to autograph. "I'd just like to ask her one thing; where's the truck she carries her heart in? Because she couldn't possibly fit it all in that little body."

Reprinted with permission—The Toronto Star Syndicate.

Who	
What	
Where	
When	
Why	
How	

Look in your local newspaper to find a news report about a local hero.
Use the 5 W's and How to give a friend an oral summary of your hero.

The children will: □ interpret to obtain information in a news report □ jot to summarize a news report □ extend to find and give an oral summary of a news report

News Reports Spark Stories

Read these beginnings of newspaper reports.

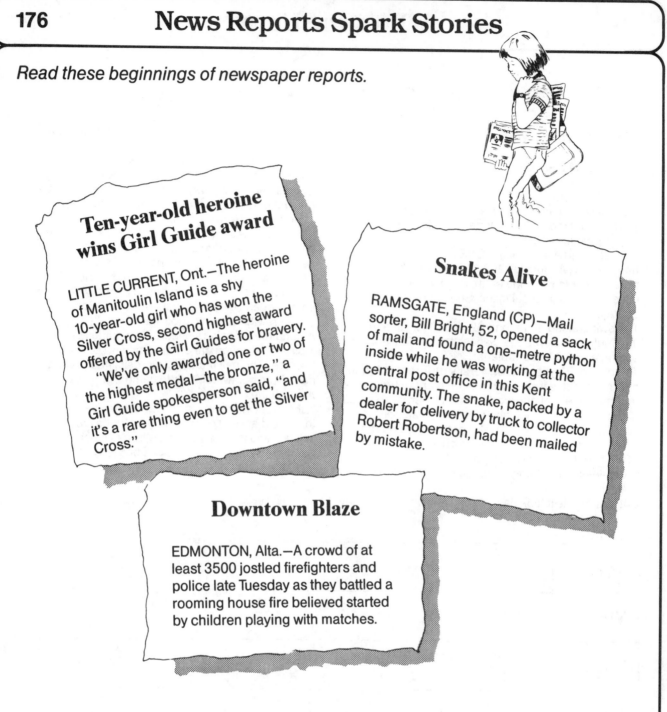

Ten-year-old heroine wins Girl Guide award

LITTLE CURRENT, Ont.—The heroine of Manitoulin Island is a shy 10-year-old girl who has won the Silver Cross, second highest award offered by the Girl Guides for bravery. "We've only awarded one or two of the highest medal—the bronze," a Girl Guide spokesperson said, "and it's a rare thing even to get the Silver Cross."

Snakes Alive

RAMSGATE, England (CP)—Mail sorter, Bill Bright, 52, opened a sack of mail and found a one-metre python inside while he was working at the central post office in this Kent community. The snake, packed by a dealer for delivery by truck to collector Robert Robertson, had been mailed by mistake.

Downtown Blaze

EDMONTON, Alta.—A crowd of at least 3500 jostled firefighters and police late Tuesday as they battled a rooming house fire believed started by children playing with matches.

Choose one to use as a 'starter' for your own story.

Think about these kinds of questions as you plan your story.

Who are the characters? What characters would you change or add?
What details in the news report would you change or add?
What events happened before the report? What will happen after?

Share your completed story with some friends.

The children will: ☐ choose to identify a writing topic   ☐ write to develop a story

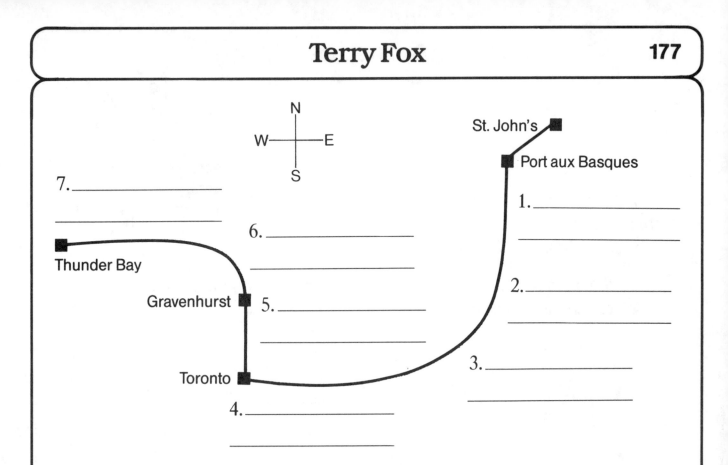

7._____

_____

6._____

_____

5._____

_____

4._____

_____

1._____

_____

2._____

_____

3._____

_____

St. John's

Port aux Basques

Thunder Bay

Gravenhurst

Toronto

Put these events in the correct order on the map.

- Cancer Society volunteers collect cash in green garbage bags.

- 10 000 citizens donate $10 000.

- Terry asks to be taken to the hospital.

- Terry runs through howling winds and pouring rain.

- Terry is joined by 10-year-old Greg Scott.

- Terry writes in his diary, "Today I had tremendous support."

- Terry receives a birthday telegram with 1000 signatures.

Choose one of these activities to complete.

— Write a birthday telegram for Terry.
— Illustrate one of the events.
— Give a radio report about one of the events.
— Write a journal entry for Terry or Greg Scott.

Share your activity with a friend.

The children will: □ rearrange to sequence events   □ choose to complete activities

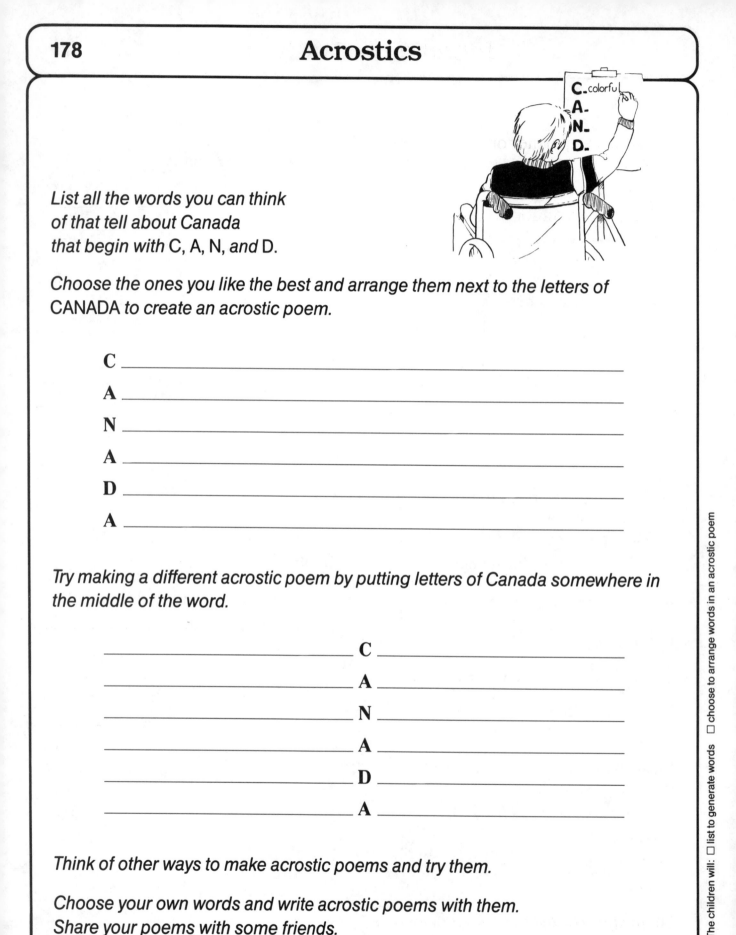

*List all the words you can think
of that tell about Canada
that begin with C, A, N, and D.*

*Choose the ones you like the best and arrange them next to the letters of
CANADA to create an acrostic poem.*

C _____

A _____

N _____

A _____

D _____

A _____

*Try making a different acrostic poem by putting letters of Canada somewhere in
the middle of the word.*

_____ **C** _____

_____ **A** _____

_____ **N** _____

_____ **A** _____

_____ **D** _____

_____ **A** _____

Think of other ways to make acrostic poems and try them.

*Choose your own words and write acrostic poems with them.
Share your poems with some friends.*

The children will: ☐ list to generate words   ☐ choose to arrange words in an acrostic poem

How to Play
—Play with a partner or a small group.
—Write a word in each space that begins with a letter at the left
  and that belongs in the category at the top.
—Set a time limit for the game.
—Score one point for each correct word.

	Flowers	Animals	Famous People	Jobs	Cities
P					
R					
O					
V					
I					
N					
C					
E					

Variations
Make up a new game. You could:
—change the word at the left.
—add to or change the categories at the top.
—write as many words as possible in each space.
—make up different rules.

Challenge your friends to play your new game.

The children will: ☐ list to classify words   ☐ expand to create a new game

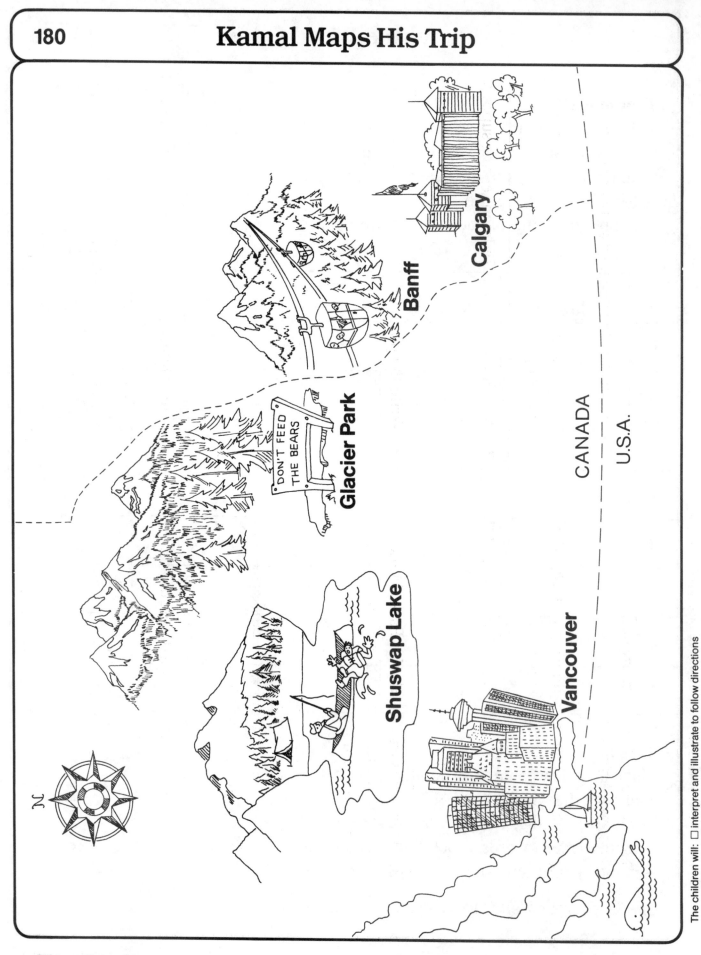

The children will: ☐ interpret and illustrate to follow directions

The children will: ☐ interpret and illustrate to follow directions ☐ choose to complete activities

Follow the directions to show how Kamal completed his sketch map.

1. Mark an X where Kamal's trip starts. Mark his first day's travel with a green line.

2. Kamal has just fallen out of his canoe while trying to catch a fish. Draw a picture of the fish that got away.

3. He is on his way to Glacier Park. Mark Kamal's route in red. Draw a tent to show where he camped.

4. Kamal is on top of a mountain in Banff. Draw a river in blue that is flowing to the Pacific Ocean. Draw three circles to show where he saw the bears.

5. He arrives in Calgary and goes to the Prehistoric Park. Draw a dinosaur that he saw.

6. Draw the route in yellow that he would take to get home.

Choose two of these activities to complete.

1. Make a list of the things that you would take on a camping trip.

2. Draw Kamal and the Tadmans eating supper.

3. Write the postcard that Kamal sent to Yamina.

4. Write a paragraph describing Kamal's gondola ride.

5. Find out the meanings of the words that Kamal learned and explain them to a friend.

6. Be Kamal and retell the story of your trip to a partner.

All Aboard!

Work with a partner to read the train schedule and answer the questions.

km	mi.	Day	Time	Station
0	0	1	16:30	DP Montreal
285	177		19:31	Kingston
539	335		22:10	AR Toronto
		2	23:59	DP Toronto
965	600		07:30	AR Sudbury
			08:05	DP Sudbury
1229	764		12:30	Devon
1854	1152	3	00:40	AR Thunder Bay
			01:15	DP Thunder Bay
2325	1445		07:00	Kenora
2528	1571		10:00	AR Winnipeg
			13:30	DP Winnipeg

How many days does it take to get from Montreal to Winnipeg? _____

How far is it in kilometres? _____

Find the two stations that are the closest together.
How many kilometres are between them? _____

Choose two other stations. How far is it between them? _____

How long does it take to travel that distance? _____

How long does the train stay in Winnipeg? _____

*Plan a trip from Montreal to Winnipeg. Decide where you will get off
the train and how long you will stay. Give all your arrival and departure times.
Share your holiday plans with other classmates.*

The children will: ☐ interpret to identify and infer information in a train schedule

There is a place in Canada that is famous for something very special—wild horses.

Out in the Atlantic Ocean, off the coast of Nova Scotia, there is a lonely place called Sable Island. The island is not much more than a sandbar. There are no trees, only sand dunes covered with beach grasses, with a few fresh-water ponds and cranberry bogs in the hollows.

In times past there had been hundreds of shipwrecks along the island's windswept and foggy shores. And that may be how wild horses came to be there. Perhaps many years ago a few horses escaped the sinking ships and the stormy sea, and managed to reach the beaches. Now about thirty to forty small family herds make Sable Island their home.

A young stallion called Seafire is one of these island horses. He is the color of the sun rising over the sea and has a spirit to match.

Until last spring, Seafire spent most of his time alone. He watched the other horses from a distance and wandered the dunes learning about the island. He explored the hills and hollows, and discovered the freshwater ponds. He ambled about, ankle deep among the waterweeds, peacefully nibbling the new shoots. But as the days grew longer and warmer, Seafire became more interested in the other horses and began to follow the small groups closely.

Then with mid-summer a whole new kind of life began for the young stallion. Several mares joined him, and so Seafire had a family herd of his own.

The small herd spent the rest of the summer together, enjoying the warm days and the rich green plants. One of the mares, who was older and more experienced, led the group from place to place, to wherever she recalled that good food or shelter could be found.

As for Seafire, his carefree days of wandering over the dunes and dozing in the summer sunshine were over. It was up to him to keep the herd together. While the senior mare led the group into pastures of beach grass, he followed along watchfully, snatching mouthfuls of grass as he looked out for intruders. More often than not there would be another stallion ready to challenge Seafire and try to steal his mares away.

One stallion, older and bigger than Seafire, was a particular nuisance. His name was Northwind. Whenever Northwind appeared, Seafire would dash over to meet him and the two horses would dance about, smell each other and push and shove. If that didn't sort out who was who, a kick or two would settle the matter. But peace would only last a while. Each time Seafire just managed to drive Northwind away. But Northwind returned again and again throughout the summer to bother Seafire and the mares.

As winter approached, the lush green pastures turned to fields of poor hay and straw. Rainstorms came with the cold northwest winds, and day after day Seafire's family became more wet and miserable. Led by the senior mare, the herd went from here to there looking for better food and places to hide from the wild sea winds.

The horses found some protection in the hollows between the sandy dunes. Standing close to the sandy walls, they would wait for the worst of the storms to pass. As the horses of Sable Island did every winter, Seafire and the mares had grown thick, woolly coats to keep themselves a little warmer, but even so, they were very uncomfortable.

Then the snow came, ___1___ along with it freezing ___2___ . Blowing sand and snow ___3___ the horses and stung ___4___ eyes. The senior mare ___5___ the herd close together ___6___ warmth. It was the ___7___ they could do.

This ___8___ one of the hardest Sable Island ___9___ in many years. The ___10___ grass made such poor ___11___ that to have enough ___12___ to keep warm, the ___13___ had to depend upon ___14___ reserved strength they had ___15___ up over the summer. ___16___ was a very long ___17___ , and those that were ___18___ poorest condition could not ___19___ .

Finally spring arrived. Seafire ___20___ the mares were thin ___21___ weak, and very tired. ___22___ they were all alive!

___23___ the sun shone they ___24___ stand about happily soaking ___25___ the warmth. And as ___26___ sun shone more often, ___27___ began to lose their ___28___ coats. The grasses grew ___29___ at first, but eventually ___30___ up tall and green, ___31___ there were fine pastures ___32___ again.

But Seafire's troubles ___33___ not over yet. So ___34___ horses had died over ___35___ winter that there were ___36___ number of stallions on island without herds, and ___37___ of the ___38___ younger horses ___39___ not have experienced mares ___40___ guide them. What an uproar this caused on Sable Island! Horses galloped about, chasing and fighting each other.

There were many challenges and threats and very few agreements. Seafire was kept so busy guarding his mares he got very little rest.

Then, one day, Northwind, who hadn't been seen since the summer before, arrived as big and bold as ever. Seafire dashed to meet him and keep him away from the herd. Northwind pranced and pushed, Seafire reared and threatened. But Seafire was no longer the young and inexperienced stallion of the previous summer. Suddenly the fight seemed too much for Northwind and off he galloped, over the dunes and away!

Northwind never came back to bother Seafire again. Although he would be challenged by many other stallions in the future, Seafire was able to protect his family. He knew it, Northwind knew it, and the mares were sure of it!

Reprinted from *The Wild Horses of Sable Island* by Zoe Lucas with permission of the publisher, Greey de Pencier Books.

Amos &
Boris &
Paddington
Too

Animal Tales

 1. Look through picture books and illustrated stories about animals. Choose the books with pictures that you like the best and make a display for your classroom. You might wish to choose one story and find out how different artists illustrated that story. Or you might choose books about one animal only and find out how different artists illustrated that animal. Or you might choose books about a variety of animals.

2. Compile a bibliography of animal tales. You may wish to choose one category of animals such as pig tales, horse tales, or cat tales, and find books that fit that category. Or you may prefer to think of an age level, and choose books for that age group. What kind of list could you develop for a grade one class, a grade two class, a grade four class?

3. Find an animal tale that is told on a record or tape. Play it for some friends. Talk about how the story "comes alive" when you listen to it. Did only one person narrate the story or was there more than one performer? Did the performer use music or other sound effects?

4. Make a certificate of merit for your favorite animal character, animal story, or author of animal tales. Include what the certificate is for and why it is being awarded. Post your certificate in the classroom or the library, or send your certificate to the author or publisher of the book.

The children will: ☐ choose to complete unit activities

5. What would happen if Charlotte the spider met Paddington the bear? Work with a partner to write or act out a dialogue between two animal characters from different tales. Tape record your dialogue and play it for some classmates.

6. List the names of as many animal characters as you can think of. Write the titles of the stories, poems, or books they come from, and the kind of animal they are. Use your list to make a book of animal characters—or make up an animal character name game for your classmates to play.

7. Many animal tales are written from the point of view of a person. Choose a story or part of a story that is written this way and rewrite it from the point of view of the animal. Read your "new" story to some friends. Can they guess what story it is?

8. Interview some classmates about their favorite animal tales. You might wish to find out their favorite animal character, favorite animal book, and favorite author of animal stories. Share your information from the interviews with your class.

9. Work with a group of friends to plan an animal tale book day. You might like to dress up as your favorite animal character. As your character you could read aloud part of your tale, or dramatize a scene from the book, or tell about your life, or . . .

10. Find an animal tale book in your library. Here are some you might enjoy reading.

> *The Cat in the Cathedral,* by Bernadette Renaud.
> *The Cricket in Times Square,* by George Selden.
> *The Dog Who Wouldn't Be,* by Farley Mowat.
> *The Mouse and the Motorcycle,* by Beverly Cleary.
> *The Velveteen Rabbit,* by Margery Williams.
> *Stuart Little,* by E.B. White.
> *Zoom Away,* by Tim Wynne-Jones.

The children will: ☐ choose to complete unit activities

Where Did that Name Come From?

The sandwich has been popular for nearly two hundred years. It was named for its inventor, the Earl of Sandwich.

The Earl lived in England during the 1700s, and he was known throughout the country for his love of gambling. One evening, he played a gambling game with a group of friends. There was a lot of prize money to win, and they gambled through the night, not bothering to eat. By early morning they were all very hungry, but the Earl of Sandwich refused to stop the game. Instead, he ordered a servant to bring everyone slices of cold beef between two pieces of bread so they could eat with their fingers while they continued to play. And so, the sandwich was born.

Do you have a jacket or a sweater with raglan sleeves? This type of sleeve first appeared in 1898 on a new style of overcoat.

The coat was called a Raglan to honor a famous British soldier, Lord Raglan, who fought with the Duke of Wellington.

The sleeves in other overcoats were sewn into armholes. Raglan sleeves, however, were sewn right to the collar seam of the coat, so there were no seams across the shoulders where rain might seep through. This feature made Raglan overcoats very popular in England.

The Raglan overcoat is no longer made. But if you look at current fashions, you will still see raglan sleeves on many styles of clothes we wear today.

Choose two or three things from this list and find out how they got their names:
cardigan, mackintosh, jeans, saxophone, peach melba, teddy bear, frankfurter,
hamburger.
Share your information with some friends.

The children will: □ interpret to obtain information   □ research to obtain information

Make a list of people and things you might see on the platform at Paddington Station.

_____   _____   _____

_____   _____   _____

_____   _____   _____

_____   _____   _____

_____   _____   _____

Choose items from your list to draw a map of the platform.
Label each item.

EXIT

RAILWAY TRACKS

Share your map with some friends.

The children will: ☐ list to generate ideas   ☐ map to organize details

Paddington's Report Card

Complete the report card on Paddington's behavior and share it with a friend.

Behavior	Mark	Comments
Manners		
Honesty		
Co-operation		
Willingness to Learn		

General Comments

_____

_____

_____

_____

_____

_____

Make a report card for another animal character in a story or poem.

The children will: ☐ extend to create a report card

Complete the chart by jotting what each character is like and how you know.

Fern		Mr. Arable	
Characteristics	Proofs	Characteristics	Proofs

Mrs. Arable		Avery	
Characteristics	Proofs	Characteristics	Proofs

Share your chart with some classmates.
Discuss whether you would like to know any of the characters and tell why or why not.

Wol Learns to Fly

Draw cartoons of the next five most important events, in the correct order. Write a caption for each cartoon.

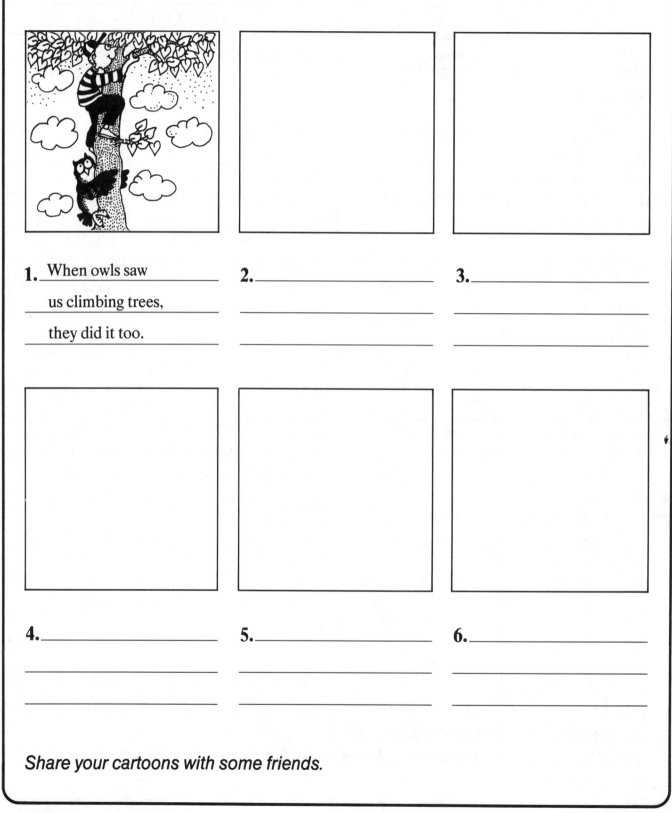

1. When owls saw us climbing trees, they did it too.

2._____

3._____

4._____

5._____

6._____

Share your cartoons with some friends.

The children will: ☐ illustrate to sequence events ☐ jot to write captions

A small Peruvian bear gets lost in Paddington Station.

An owl named Wol learns to fly.

A spider spins messages in her webs to save a pig's life.

These situations all come from famous animal tales, but do you think the tales tell the same kind of story? Here are categories that some book reviewers use to describe different kinds of animal tales.

In stories like *A Bear Called Paddington,* the animals can feel and say and do all the things that people can. Ralph the mouse rides a shiny motorcycle in *The Mouse and the Motorcycle* by Beverly Cleary, and a moose becomes a headwaiter in a restaurant in *The Blue Moose* by Daniel Pinkwater. Stories like these are animal fantasies, and they are one of the most popular kinds of animal stories. Here are the titles of some other animal fantasies: *The Mousewife* by Rumer Godden, *Zoom Away* by Tim Wynne-Jones, *Stuart Little* by E.B. White, *The Cricket in Times Square* by George Selden.

Owls in the Family is a very different kind of animal story because its animal characters behave like real animals. Orphaned baby owls raised by people would imitate their human masters. Realistic animal stories can be about pets or wild animals. *The Cat in the Cathedral* by Bernadette Renaud is about an independent stray cat and a church organist;

The Midnight Fox by Betsy Byars is about a boy who spends a summer watching a mother fox and her cubs in the woods. Some realistic animal tales you might enjoy are: *Beautiful Joe* by Marshall Saunders, *Misty of Chincoteague* by Marguerite Henry, *The House of Wings* by Betsy Byars, *The Dog Who Wouldn't Be* by Farley Mowat, *Gentle Ben* by Walt Morey.

Charlotte's Web is a mixture of fantastic and realistic animals. Wilbur and Charlotte don't live in houses or dress up or ride around in cars. They behave like real animals, except for one thing—they can talk. Another animal story like this is *The Tough Winter* by Robert Lawson. George the rabbit and his family live in burrows, just like real rabbits, but they also talk, tell stories, and even crack jokes! The same thing is true in *The Animals of Farthing Wood* by Colin Dann, in which the animals hold meetings and plan a journey to a new and safer home. Some more talking animal stories are: *The Acorn Quest* by Jane Yolen, *The Bat Poet* by Randall Jarrell, *Bunnicula* by Deborah Howe and James Howe, *A Whale Called Henry* by M. Wylie Blanchet.

It doesn't really matter whether you like fantasy animals best, or talking animals. Maybe you love all three kinds! Just start reading and you're sure to find tail tales that are just right for you.

Underline the parts of the article that tell about the three categories. Work with a partner to make a chart for the categories and titles of stories from the article. Revisit the animal stories in Springboards *and* Tickle the Sun *and list them in your chart. Add any other animal stories that you know to the categories.*

The children will: ☐ underline to identify main ideas ☐ chart to classify information ☐ revisit to expand a chart

My Gumbie Cat

Complete the verses to make your own poem.

But when the day's hustle and bustle is done,

_____

And when all the family's in bed and asleep,

_____

She is deeply concerned with the ways of the mice—

_____

So when she has got them lined up on the matting,

_____

But when the day's hustle and bustle is done,

_____

As she finds that the mice will not ever keep quiet,

_____

And believing that nothing is done without trying,

_____

She makes them a mouse-cake of bread and dried peas,

_____

Share your verses with your friends.

The children will: ☐ write to complete a poem

Read the paragraph and think of possible describing words for each blank.

One night, in a ___1___ sea, he marvelled at the sight of some whales spouting ___2___ water; and later, lying on the deck of his boat gazing at the ___3___, starry sky, the ___4___ mouse Amos, a little speck of a living thing in the ___5___ living universe, felt thoroughly akin to it all. ___6___ by the beauty and mystery of everything, he rolled over and over and right off the deck of his boat and into the sea.

List possible words that would make sense for each blank.

1	2	3

4	5	6

Share your words with a partner. Then read the paragraph on pages 376-377 of "Amos & Boris" to find the exact words the author used. Write the exact words in the boxes.

The children will: ☐ hypothesize to predict and confirm descriptive words

Numerous Humorous Words

Work with a partner to write examples for each category.

Alliteration: _____

_____

_____

_____

Rhymes: _____

_____

_____

_____

Nonsense Words: _____

_____

_____

_____

Repetition: _____

_____

_____

_____

Write other examples from poems or stories you have read.
Share your examples with your classmates.

The children will: ☐ classify to identify humorous words

Use the pictures, captions, and any other information you know to write a just-so story about one of these animals.

Red Kangaroo

—male called "boomer", female called "flyer", baby called "joey"
—joey lives in mother's pouch for 6 months
—males are bright maroon with white faces

Platypus

—has bill like a duck, webbed feet, but not a bird
—lays eggs with soft, leathery shells
—paddled-shape tail helps it swim

Emu

—is a bird but can't fly
—can run up to 30 kilometres per hour
—male usually incubates eggs
—has two feathers growing from each skin opening

Koala Bear

—looks like a bear but isn't
—baby rides in mother's pouch until 8 months old
—eats only certain kinds of eucalyptus leaves

Read the tale to compare it with "How the World Got Wisdom."

In the village of Akim there was once a fisherman who worked very hard. Every morning he gathered his nets into his long boat or set his traps in the river. Sometimes, even at night, the fisherman went far out into the sea, and when he returned he mended his nets and cleaned his boat. Spider noticed how hard the fisherman worked. But he also noticed how many big fish the fisherman brought to his house each evening, and what a feast the fisherman's family had. Spider was determined to find a way to get some of the fish for himself, and so one day he went to see the fisherman and offered to help him.

Now, of course, Spider did not intend to do any work. He thought he could play a trick on the fisherman and get all the fish he wanted without having to work at all.

But the fisherman knew all about Spider. He knew that Spider was greedy and lazy and always up to something. Yet, when Spider asked if he could help him, the fisherman said, "Of course, you can. I will be very glad to have you help, Spider."

The people of Akim all laughed. "What a fool is the fisherman!" they said. "Spider will take all the fish and the fisherman will do all the work."

But the fisherman only smiled. "You will see," he thought to himself.

On the first morning when Spider came to help, the fisherman said to Spider, "Now let us discuss the way we will go about things. Someone has to do the work and someone has to get tired, so we will take turns. One day you will be the one who gets tired, and I will do the work.

The next day I will be the one who gets tired, and you will do the work."

"Do not talk in long sentences," answered Spider. Only talk about what we will do today."

"Very well," replied the fisherman. "Today we will make traps to catch the fish. I will make the traps and you will get tired."

"I get tired?" shouted Spider. "Indeed not. I will make the traps, and you will be the one who gets tired!"

For Spider hated to get tired more than anything.

"Very well," said the fisherman, "if that is what pleases you."

And he lay down on the ground as though he were very tired, while Spider made all the traps.

The following day the fisherman said to Spider, "My friend, today we must set the

The children will: ☐ interpret and chart to compare folk tales   ☐ summarize to note main idea

The children will: ☐ interpret and chart to compare folk tales   ☐ summarize to note main idea

traps in the river. Yesterday, you made the traps and I got tired. Today, we'll change around, I will set the traps in the river and you will get tired for me."

"Never!" shouted Spider, who hated to get tired and wanted to get some fish. "I will set the traps myself, and you will get tired."

And so Spider set the traps in the water while the fisherman lay down on the bank. Spider bent over for a long time, putting the traps deep in the water. After a while his back began to ache. All the while the fisherman lay on the bank. He watched Spider working. And while he watched he moaned and groaned and rubbed his head and rolled about as though he were very tired.

"My oh my oh my!" he cried. "I'm *so* tired." And then the fisherman went to sleep.

Well, on the third day the fisherman said to Spider, "Surely we must have a change today. It is only fair. I shall collect the fish from the traps and you will be the one who gets tired."

Now, you know Spider was planning all along to eat some of the fish.

"Do you think I am a fool?" he shouted. "What makes you think I want to get tired? You will get tired and I will collect the fish."

"If you insist," answered the fisherman. And he lay down on the bank of the river again.

When the people of Akim walked past the river, they saw Spider busily gathering fish and the fisherman lying on the bank looking

very tired. He moaned and groaned even louder than the day before, but this time he did not go to sleep. He kept his eyes fastened on Spider, so poor Spider did not get any fish at all.

On the final day, the fisherman said to Spider, "Today I really mean what I say. I will take the fish to market and you will get tired."

"Nonsense!" said Spider, "I will never agree to get tired. I will carry the fish to market and you will get tired."

And so it was, even up to the last day. Spider carried all the fish to market. The fisherman walked behind him, huffing and puffing as though he were indeed very tired. When they reached the market, Spider put the fish in a big pile.

Then the fisherman sat down beside them. When people came to buy, they paid the fisherman, for was he not the only fisherman, and did not the fish belong to him?

When all the fish were gone, the fisherman gave Spider four coins, one for each day he had worked. Spider saw that he had been tricked instead of tricking the fisherman. He had very little of the money and none of the fish. At first he was angry, and then, as he was in the habit of doing, he simply burst out laughing at himself.

"Next time I will be the winner," he said. And he went merrily back to his little house among the banana leaves.

Excerpt from *The Adventures of Spider* retold by Joyce Cooper Arkhurst. Copyright © 1964 by Joyce Cooper Arkhurst. Reprinted by permission of Little, Brown and Company.

Work with a partner to organize your comparisons in a chart that will tell about the characters, and events, and ending of each folk tale.
Write a moral for each tale.

The Boy and the Bears

Complete the chart.

How the bears behaved like boys	How the boy behaved like bears

Use the chart to help you answer these questions. Discuss your answers with a friend.

How did the boy benefit from living with the bears?
Do you think the bears benefited from living with the boy? Why or why not?

The children will: ☐ chart to classify animal and human behavior   ☐ talk to infer and explain conclusions

Read each group of sentences and try different ways of combining them into one sentence. Write the sentence that you think sounds the best. Compare your sentences with the ones the author used.

1. He walked a great distance.
   He saw the light of a wigwam.

   _____

   _____

2. He had slept all winter in the den of the bears.
   He felt no different than if he had slept a single night.

   _____

   _____

3. He listened carefully.
   He learned the language of the bears.
   He could converse with them.

   _____

   _____

4. The boy said good-bye to the old bear and the cubs.
   He went back through the forest to his village.
   The people had long ago decided that he was dead.

   _____

   _____

Look through your writing portfolio. Are there any sentences you could improve by combining them?

Read these tale beginnings.
How are they the same?

Once on a time when wishes were aplenty, a fisherman and his wife lived by the side of the sea. All that they ate came out of the sea.

(Greyling)

Once in another time, my friends, an old woman called Tante Odette lived in Canada. She was a plump little woman with beady, black eyes, a pouf of a moustache and a double chin.

(The Skunk in Tante Odette's Oven)

Once upon a time, there was an old king who had three sons. There came a time when the king knew that he would soon die, and so he called his three sons together and said, "I will die soon. When I am gone, look behind the stable door. There you will find an old wooden bowl. Each of you must shake it, and whatever falls out of it will be your inheritance."

(The Princess of Tomboso)

In the days of the people who are gone, there lived a small boy whose parents were dead. Having no home of his own, he lived sometimes in one wigwam and sometimes in another.

(Brother to the Bears)

Once many years ago in a country far to the east there lived a wealthy merchant. He was a widower and had an only daughter named Danina. She was dainty and beautiful, and he loved her more than he loved all of his treasures.

(The Girl Who Loved the Wind)

Millions and millions of years ago, deep down in the earth under a huge mountain, there lived an elemental and powerful gnome.

(Count Beet)

A long, long time ago, in a small country village in Japan, there lived a poor farmer and his wife, who were very good people. They had a number of children, and found it hard to feed them all.

(The Boy Who Drew Cats)

Once upon a time there was—
   "A king!" my little readers will say at once.
   No, my dears, you are wrong. Once upon a time there was a stick of wood.

(Pinocchio)

Choose one beginning and work with a friend to write your own tale.
Compare your tale with the original.
Find other tale beginnings and make a display with them.

The children will: ☐ interpret to compare folk tale beginnings ☐ choose to write a folk tale ☐ research to find and display other folk tale beginnings

Revisit the Animal Fables on pages 36 to 38 of Springboards 4.
Work with a partner and choose one of the fables to tell as a story.
Use these questions to help plan how you will tell your story.

What details can you add:
- about the characters?
- about the setting?
- about the events?

What dialogue can you add to the narration?

What new characters can you add? What new events?

Will you tell the events of the story in the same order as they happened
in the fable?
Can you rearrange the events of the story so that:
- you start with the moral?
- you start in the middle?

Will you use props of the characters or setting to help you tell the story?

Practise telling your story with your partner. Then tell it to some friends.

The children will: ☐ talk to plan and tell a story

Read what Celia Barker Lottridge says about her story, "Gerasim and the Lion."

What is "Gerasim and The Lion" about?
It's a story about not stereotyping people. Just because the lion is a big and fierce animal doesn't mean that it must have eaten the donkey. Now Gerasim is an unusual man. He looks at the lion as an individual lion and doesn't just assume that all lions are the same. But even Gerasim makes a mistake. He does think that the lion has eaten the donkey.

You say that Gerasim is an unusual man. In what ways is he unusual?
Gerasim can see that creatures are individuals and he sees the possibilities in people and animals. He does make a mistake about the lion, but when he realizes that he shouldn't have just assumed that the lion ate the donkey, he admits he was wrong. That's one of the things I love about Gerasim— when he makes a mistake, he says "I was wrong." A lot of people can't do that.
And even when he assumes that the lion has eaten the donkey he doesn't do anything harsh. He doesn't kill it or send it away. He is a just man. And he gives the lion a second chance.

Often the animals in stories can talk. Why didn't you have the lion and the donkey in your story talk?
In this story I wanted the animals to be like real animals. The stories I tell have something wonderful, some amazing thing, in the middle. In this story it is that a lion would become so attached to a person that he would stop acting like a lion. That's why the lion has to be a real lion, otherwise it wouldn't be a surprise that he would take care of a donkey. If he was a talking lion then there wouldn't be the surprise.

Discuss these questions with some friends.
Which answers do you agree with? Why?
Which answers don't you agree with? Why?
What ideas could you add to each answer?
What questions would you like to ask her?

The children will: ☐ interpret to understand author's point of view   ☐ talk to formulate and explain opinions

Read the two versions of samples from Beatrix Potter's writing.

Early Draft	Published Writing
Once upon a time there was a wood-mouse and her name was Mrs. Tittlemouse. Her house was in a bank under a hedge. Inside the house was a kitchen and a parlour, and a pantry and a larder. And there were yards and yards of sandy passages leading to store rooms and nut-cellars and seed-cellars, all amongst the roots of the hedge. And there was Mrs. Tittlemouse's bedroom, where she slept in a little box bed.	Once upon a time there was a wood-mouse, and her name was Mrs. Tittlemouse. She lived in a bank under a hedge. Such a funny house! There were yards and yards of sandy passages, leading to storerooms and nut-cellars and seed-cellars, all amongst the roots of the hedge. There was a kitchen, a parlour, a pantry, and a larder. Also, there was Mrs. Tittlemouse's bedroom, where she slept in a little box bed!
'Come! Mr. Drake Puddle-Duck,' said Moppet – 'Come and button up Tom!'	'Come! Mr. Drake Puddle-Duck,' said Moppet—'Come and help us to dress him! Come and button up Tom!'
She called them to come down, smacked them and took them back to the house.	She pulled them off the wall, smacked them, and took them back to the house.
There were very extraordinary noises during the whole of the tea-party somehow.	Somehow there were very extraordinary noises over-head; which disturbed the dignity and repose of the tea-party.

Discuss the writing with some friends. Talk about what changes Beatrix Potter made and why you think she made the changes.
Do you think the changes improved her writing?

The children will: ☐ interpret to identify and compare author's revisions   ☐ talk to explain and draw conclusions

Reading/Speaking

Snoopy Says . . .

Complete the chart to compare Beatrix Potter's ideas about writing
with your ideas about writing.

Where Beatrix got her ideas	Where I get my ideas

Works Beatrix published	Works I have published

What Beatrix says about writing	What I say about writing

Share your chart with a friend.

The children will: ☐ chart to relate author's ideas about writing to their own

Sunday afternoon Bruce and I met Mr. Miller at his house. He was a big man with a bald head. He wore short pants and carried a great big haversack full of cameras and films. He was excited about the owl's-nest, all right, and he was in such a hurry to get to it that Bruce and I had to run most of the way, just to keep up with him.

When we reached the edge of the Owl Bluff Mr. Miller got out his biggest camera and, after he had fussed with it for about half an hour, he said he was ready.

"We'll walk single file, boys," he said, "and quiet as mice. Tiptoe . . . mustn't scare the owl away."

Well, that sounded all right, only you can't walk quietly in a poplar bluff because of all the dead sticks underfoot. They crack and pop like firecrackers. Under Mr. Miller's feet they sounded like cannon shots. Anyway, when we got to the nest tree there was no sign of the owl.

"Are you sure this IS an owl's-nest?" Mr. Miller asked us.

"Yes, sir!" Bruce answered. "We seen the owl setting on it!"

Mr. Miller shuddered. "*Saw* the owl *sitting* on it, Bruce. . . . Hmmm. . . . Well—I suppose I'd better climb up and take a peek. But if you ask me, I think it's just an old crow's-nest."

He put down his big haversack and the camera, and up he went. He was wearing a big floppy hat to keep his head from getting sunburned and I don't think he could see out from under it very well.

"Boy, has he got knobby knees!" Bruce whispered to me. We both started to giggle and we were still giggling when Mr. Miller began to shout.

"Hoyee!" he yelled. "SCAT—WHOEEE! Hoy, HOY!"

Bruce and I ran around the other side of the tree so we could see up to the nest. Mr. Miller was hanging onto the tree with both arms and he was kicking out with his feet. It looked as if his feet had slipped off the branch and couldn't find a place to get hold of again. Just then there was a swooshing sound and the old owl came diving down right on top of him with her wings spread wide. She looked as big as a house and she didn't miss Mr. Miller by more than a few centimetres. Then she swooped up and away again.

Mr. Miller was yelling ___1___ strange things, and good ___2___ loud too. He finally ___3___ one foot back on ___4___ branch but he was ___5___ such a hurry to ___6___ down that he picked ___7___ small a branch. It ___8___, and he slid about ___9___ metres before his belt ___10___ on a stub. While ___11___ was trying to get ___12___, the owl came back ___13___ another try. This time ___14___ was so close that ___15___ could see her big ___16___ eyes, and both Bruce ___17___ I ducked. She had ___18___ claws stuck way out ___19___ front of her. Just ___20___ she dived toward him, Mr. Miller, ___21___ couldn't see her coming ___22___ of his hat, gave ___23___ jump upward to get ___24___ of the stub. The ___25___ was that the owl ___26___ miss him even if ___27___ wanted to. There was ___28___ awful flapping and yelling ___29___ then away went the ___30___, with Mr. Miller's hat.

___31___ don't think she really ___32___ that old hat. It ___33___ all Mr. Miller's fault ___34___ jumping at the wrong ___35___. The owl seemed to ___36___ trying to shake the ___37___ loose from her claws, ___38___ she couldn't because her ___39___ were hooked in it. ___40___ last we saw of her she was flying out over the prairie and she still had the hat.

When Mr. Miller got down out of the tree he went right to his haversack. He took out a bottle, opened it, and started to drink. His Adam's apple was going in and out like an accordion. After a while he put down the bottle and wiped his mouth. When he saw us staring at him he tried to smile.

"Cold tea," he explained. "Thirsty work—climbing trees in this hot weather."

"It was an owl's-nest, wasn't it, sir?" asked Bruce.

Mr. Miller looked at him hard for a moment. Then:

"Yes, Bruce," he said. "I guess it was."